Bible
Promises

Books by Ivor Powell

Bible Cameos
Bible Gems
Bible Highways
Bible Names of Christ
Bible Nuggets
Bible Pinnacles
Bible Promises
Bible Windows
Matthew's Majestic Gospel
Mark's Superb Gospel
Luke's Thrilling Gospel
John's Wonderful Gospel
The Amazing Acts
The Exciting Epistle to the Ephesians
David: His Life and Times
What in the World Will Happen Next?

Bible
Promises

80 Inspirational
Studies on the
Faithfulness of God

Ivor Powell

kregel
PUBLICATIONS

Grand Rapids, MI 49501

Bible Promises: 80 Inspirational Studies on the Faithfulness of God by Ivor Powell.

Published in 1993 by Kregel Publications, a division of Kregel, Inc., P.O. Box 2607, Grand Rapids, MI 49501.

Cover Photograph: Ted & Gwendolyn Brand Photography
Cover and Book Design: Alan G. Hartman

Library of Congress Cataloging-in-Publication Data
Powell, Ivor, 1910-
    Bible Promises: 80 inspirational studies on the faithfulness of God / Ivor Powell.
      p. cm.
    Includes index.
    1. God—Promises—Biblical teaching. I. Title.
BS680.P68P68   1993   220.6—dc20   93-1921
                                          CIP

ISBN 0-8254-3542-0 (paperback)

1 2 3 4 5 Printing / Year 97 96 95 94 93

Printed in the United States of America

CONTENTS

SECTION ONE
Great Promises For Special Occasions

SECTION TWO
Conditional Promises

5

SECTION THREE
Unconditional Promises

SECTION FOUR
Promises Awaiting Fulfillment

AUTHOR'S PREFACE

At the close of a meeting at a pastors' conference in Georgia, a young man came to me and said, "Sir, I want to thank you." I smiled and listened as he continued. "I am a Baptist preacher, but unfortunately I was unable to go to a college. I was too poor, and consequently I have very little education. But, Sir, I love to preach the Gospel, and when a congregation asked me to become their minister, I gladly accepted the invitation." He paused for a few minutes and then continued, "But it was too hard for me with my limited knowledge. Then, I discovered your books, and they changed everything! Now, Sir, I am preaching your sermons. You not only teach me what to say, you show me how to say it! Sir, I am grateful."

When I listened to that dedicated young minister, I knew how the Lord felt when He looked at the rich young ruler and loved him. I know of many other pastors who could give similar testimonies. Their friendship and appreciation supplied the incentive to produce this volume. It is my fervent prayer that *Bible Promises* will help many preachers of the Gospel.

This book divides into four different sections. There are promises for special occasions, conditional promises, unconditional promises, and promises awaiting fulfillment. The most exciting section deals with promises awaiting fulfillment. I confess that writing this volume blessed my soul.

I would like to thank Kregel Publications of Grand Rapids, Michigan. My friends in the Kregel family have been an inspiration to me. They are people who enrich Christians around the world. I dedicate this book to the pastors for whom the messages were produced. May God bless them!

IVOR POWELL

Santa Barbara, California
September, 1993

8

Great Promises For Special Occasions

"And him that cometh unto me I will in no wise cast out."

I shall never forget a delightful lady in Scotland who listened as I explained the Gospel, and then exclaimed, "I know all that, but I do not *feel* saved." I tried to explain that when Christ said "Whosoever will, may come," He included her in His great invitation. Yet it did not matter what I said, she always answered, "It is useless. I do not *feel* saved." It appeared that if she could have experienced an electric shock, it might have strengthened her faith. James said, "Faith without works is dead" (James 2:20), but my friend countered that statement with one of her own, "Faith without feeling is useless."

Faith is more important than feelings. A man may be deliriously happy, exuberant with praise, and ecstatic about his religious experiences, but if at the Day of Judgment God rejected him, his feelings would be inconsequential (Matt. 7:21–23). On the other hand, a man may be depressed about his spiritual condition, but, if God welcomes him into the everlasting kingdom, doubt cannot prevent his entry. What God says is more important than feelings.

When God accepts a man, that person *is* accepted whether or not he believes it to be true. If God rejects a man, that soul is lost in spite of anything he may feel or say. Human emotions can change dramatically, but the Word of God is changeless and abides forever. To be saved a sinner must come to Christ, and when he does, nothing in time or eternity can prevent his being accepted. To doubt that promise is to dishonor God and destroy one's own happiness.

The Message of Forgiveness . . . *Converts Come to Christ*

"And when he (Jesus) saw their faith, he said unto him (the man with the palsy), Man, thy sins are forgiven thee" (Luke 5:20). The story of this text was remarkable, for apparently the sick man did not ask for forgiveness. He was brought by his friends in quest of healing. When the Lord saw their faith, He announced that the sinner had been forgiven. He did not promise to pardon the man at some future occasion. Christ forgave him instantly. The complaint of the assembled rabbis was understandable, for according to the law what Jesus did was unprecedented. The miracle which the Lord performed endorsed His testimony. The man *was* forgiven.

The Means of Forgiveness . . . *Converts Love Christ*

"And he said unto her, Thy sins are forgiven" (Luke 7:48). She was a woman of the street, but she had access to the homes of important people. Probably she had often visited that home and had purchased favors with immoral actions. Yet on that occasion, she was there for a different reason. Somewhere she had heard the Teacher from Nazareth, and His words had transformed her desires. When she bathed the feet of Jesus and used her hair as a towel, when her tears expressed the intent of her soul, the Pharisees condemned her. Nevertheless, the story told by Jesus revealed the sincerity of her repentance. It would have been impossible for Christ *not to forgive* one whose devotion was so evident.

The Majesty of Forgiveness . . . *Converts Look to Christ*

"And Jesus said unto him (the thief), Verily I say unto thee, Today shalt thou be with me in paradise" (Luke 23:43). It is interesting to note that the criminal did not ask for forgiveness. Yet none can deny he was pardoned, for otherwise he would not have accompanied the Lord to paradise. Suppose someone had asked, "But how can you be sure of this?" The thief could have replied, "Do not be ridiculous. I have the Lord's word for it, and He knows what He is talking about." That Savior has never changed.

The Miracle of Forgiveness . . . *Converts Serve Christ*

Writing to his friends John said, "I write unto you, little children, because your sins *are forgiven* for his name's sake" (1 John 2:12). The recipients of God's grace had united with other believers, and an assembly had been formed. Together those early Christians served their Lord and preached His message to the people of their generation. It is interesting to discover that in John's epistles the verb *to know* is used at least twenty-seven times. Charles Haddon Spurgeon said, "If there were one soul in hell upon whom were the marks of the blood of Jesus, all Heaven would be off to the rescue." Remember the words of the familiar chorus:

> Only believe, only believe,
> All things are possible,
> Only believe.

12

*"But I have prayed for thee, that thy faith fail not; and
when thou art converted, strengthen thy brethren."*

There is nothing more distressing than a feeling of failure. The realization that you have disappointed the Lord, your family, friends, and acquaintances is heart-breaking. The pain is accentuated by the knowledge it happened because of personal pride and over-confidence. The memory that God's warnings were disregarded when we said "It could never happen to me" is devastating.

Simon Peter provided the most prominent example of that type of person. When Luke described how the apostle "went out and wept bitterly," he expressed in one sentence the collapse of Simon's ego. Peter was always an enthusiastic disciple, but his reply to the Lord's warning was indicative of his character. Jesus said to him, "Simon, Simon, behold, Satan hath desired to have you, that he may sift you as wheat" (Luke 22:31). Peter replied, in so many words, "Lord, you need not worry about me. I am ready to go with you, both into prison and to death. That could never happen to me!" No man could doubt his sincerity. Peter meant every word he uttered. Unfortunately, circumstances change things, and Peter's brash statement was soon to be challenged.

There was a great difference between looking into the face of Jesus and staring into the tantalizing eyes of the maiden by the soldiers' fire. It was one thing to be boastful in the presence of other believers, but the true test of Peter's loyalty would come when he was surrounded by enemies. Perhaps there was rebellion in Peter's soul when he overlooked the other words of Jesus. "But I have prayed for thee, that thy faith fail not." Later, when remorse broke his heart and tears ran down his face, Peter believed himself to be the most despicable man on earth. Many people share that experience, and shame is often the greatest hindrance to returning to active service for Christ.

God's Grace Is Greater Than Our Guilt

It is possible that someone will read these words and be haunted by memories. Perhaps a sense of shame has ruined his or her service in God's kingdom, and perhaps other people also suffered. To

13

a degree, the captive Jews in Babylon knew that experience, for one of their number wrote, "By the rivers of Babylon, there we sat down, yea, we wept, when we remembered Zion" (Ps. 137:1). To live with past failures is a cross too heavy to be carried. The Lord knew about Peter's failure even before it happened, but that knowledge never impaired His love for the over-confident follower. Instead of criticizing Peter, Jesus prayed for him.

God's Desire Is More Important Than Our Distress

In his distress, Peter probably believed his ministry had ended when it was only beginning. The Lord knew his prayer would be answered and mentioned Simon's future ministry. "When thou art converted [turned back again], strengthen thy brethren." Sometimes it is difficult to forgive ourselves. Nevertheless, nothing should ever prevent our obedience to the Lord's call for reconsecration. After the resurrection of Jesus, an angel commissioned Mary saying, "But go your way, tell his disciples *and Peter* that he goeth before you into Galilee: there shall ye see him" (Mark 16:7). It seems the despondent disciple had no intention of returning, and it became necessary for the Lord to go in search of his follower (see Luke 24:34). Has He been searching for us?

God's Forgiveness Is More Attractive Than Our Failure

It would have been a tragedy if Peter had refused to respond to the entreaties of his Master. If he had stayed away, who would have been God's spokesman on the Day of Pentecost? Thousands of listeners praised the Lord when they heard the good news from the lips of the man who had failed badly. To dwell upon former failure is distressing. To persist in doing so can easily become sinful—especially when the Lord continues to call for the renewal of one's vows.

Jonah made a mistake, but he recovered and returned. Simon Peter made a mistake, but he also atoned for his failure. John Mark left his colleagues, but he also recovered and served Christ faithfully. If we feel ashamed of former failure, we should remember mistakes may become stepping stones to greater heights of achievement.

14

"This is a faithful saying, and worthy of all acceptation, that Christ Jesus came into the world to save sinners; of whom I am chief."

A man who is completely satisfied and without ambition has outlived his usefulness. When complacency continues, challenge loses its power. Sometimes failure is the source of determination to try again. When Paul in his prison in Rome reviewed his life, he concluded he was the chief of sinners, but he was mistaken in his deduction. Every sincere Christian would question his statement, saying, "He never knew me!"

A Definite Mistake

Paul was not the chief of sinners, but he thought he was! Two statements summarize the life of the apostle. Writing to arrogant people in the Philippian church, he expressed the conviction that he had reason to boast more than any of his readers. Yet he regarded his achievements as refuse. He stated the astonishing fact that as "touching the righteousness which is in the law, [I was] blameless" (Phil. 3:6). It seems evident that he was one of the best people on earth. Later in his life he explained that what had been done, was done "ignorantly, in unbelief" (1 Tim. 1:13).

When he became a Christian, his life was completely changed, and thereafter he strove continually to have "a conscience void of offense" (Acts 24:16). A man with those qualifications could never be the chief of sinners. Nevertheless, Paul believed he was and did not hesitate to claim that dubious distinction. He was approaching the Light of the World, and in that radiance it was easy to see the blemishes on his record. A man in total darkness sees nothing!

A Different Message

Paul believed the Gospel to be unique! Other messages were being preached, but only the message of Christ was "a faithful saying and worthy of all acceptation." The Romans taught that might was right, but they left slaves in chains. They believed their emperor was a god, but his conduct was a source of horror. The Sadducees believed death was the end of existence. When they died, they died as dogs and had no hope of anything eternal. The Pharisees believed in survival and claimed it depended on personal

15

merit. They created innumerable laws which enslaved men. The Greeks worshiped many gods but were never sure of anything. That was the reason why Paul at Mars Hill in Athens drew attention to an altar erected to THE UNKNOWN GOD. The Athenians were never sure if a forgotten god might be offended, and they became prey to their own fear. None of those messages met the need of the human heart, and consequently Paul affirmed that only the Gospel was "a faithful message worthy of acceptance." It offered a message not found in the religious cults of his generation.

A Delightful Mission

"Christ Jesus came into the world to save sinners." The Lord was not a political hero who had risen from among men. He had descended from heaven where He had been the King of the angels. *He came!* That signified pre-existence and a definite act of His own volition. He chose to come to earth. Three facts appear to be obvious: (1) Christ's purpose—He came. (2) Christ's patience—He endured. (3) Christ's power—He rose again to complete His assignment. The Gospel of Christ offered, above all else, assurance of sins forgiven, continuing help through life, and an abundant entrance into a life which had no end (see 2 Peter 1:11).

No other message could relate to the promises of God. Paul would have agreed with the poet who wrote, "Jesus is all we need." If for no other reason, the message of Christ was worthy of all acceptance. There was no longer a reason for any person to rest upon his or her questionable worthiness; everyone could depend upon the finished work of the Son of God.

A Dependable Christ

When Paul wrote his letters to Timothy, he was a prisoner in Rome either in a cell or in his own rented house (see Acts 28:30). Behind him lay a lifetime of valiant service. He had endured many difficulties and had suffered as much as any other Christian. His testimony to the faithfulness of God never wavered. His fellowship with Christ remained unbroken.

Obeying the command to take the Gospel to the Gentiles, Paul evangelized the world of his time within a few years. He preached to all types of people, but the strength of his ministry was the abiding presence of the risen Christ. His conduct reflected the high standards of spiritual morality set forth in his doctrines. He lived an exemplary life and was able to write, "Howbeit for this cause I obtained mercy, that in me first Jesus Christ might shew forth all longsuffering, for a pattern to them which should hereafter believe on him to life everlasting" (1 Tim. 1:16). It is far better to say you are the greatest sinner than to believe you are the greatest saint.

WHEN YOU ARE WORRIED ABOUT YOUR
PAST, REMEMBER JEREMIAH 31:34

"I will forgive their iniquity, and I will remember their sin no more."

A guilty conscience is a terrible companion whose voice cannot be silenced. Its owner may try to quiet the nagging accusations, but from beginning to end the effort is useless. Sleep becomes elusive, and nights appear to be endless when a troubled soul wrestles with problems of guilt.

I knew a Christian lady who suffered mental anguish because of her inability to forget what she had done in her youth. She believed in the Savior and rejoiced in the greatness of His salvation, but each time she remembered deeds performed in earlier years, she was overwhelmed by remorse. One day another lady said, "There is no need to worry about those sins. God has blotted them out." Her reply was instantaneous, "Oh no, those sins will never be forgiven, nor forgotten—never!" Unfortunately, that troubled woman never intended to forgive herself.

Nevertheless, the promise made by God to His people will never change. "I will forgive their iniquity, and I will remember their sin no more." When God forgives, He forgets! If the Lord has buried our sins, we should never dig them up again.

The Greatness of His Promise

This promise was given to the Hebrew nation, and it supplied an insight into the nature of the Almighty. The prophet Micah wrote, "Who is a God like unto thee, that pardoneth iniquity, and passeth by the transgression of the remnant of his heritage? he retaineth not his anger for ever, because he delighteth in mercy" (Mic. 7:18). Israel had committed many abominable errors, but there were no restrictive limits to the mercy of the Lord. There were no strings attached when He said, "I will remember their sin no more."

Since God has promised to forget our mistakes, we should use our failures as stepping stones to greater heights of efficiency. Simon Peter turned the nightmare of an agonizing defeat into the glorious triumph of a personal Pentecost.

The Guarantee of His Promise

Jeremiah wrote, "Thus saith the LORD, which giveth the sun for a light by day, and the ordinances of the moon and of the stars for

18

a light by night, which divideth the sea when the waves thereof roar; . . . if those ordinances depart from before me, saith the LORD, then the seed of Israel also shall cease from being a nation before me for ever" (Jer. 31:35–37). God holds the firmament in His hands, and the same sun and moon which shone upon Adam and Eve continue to shine upon us. These features have remained from the beginning of time and will continue to do so. The promises of God are equally reliable. They cannot fail, and that means our sins can never be resurrected.

The Gladness of His Promise

Perhaps David had similar thoughts when he wrote the fourth psalm, "Thou hast enlarged me when I was in distress; have mercy upon me and hear my prayer . . . Thou hast put gladness in my heart . . . I will both lay me down in peace and sleep: for thou, LORD, only makest me dwell in safety" (vv. 1, 7,8). The sweet singer of Israel often disappointed God, but the compassion of the Lord never failed.

When David repented of his sins, he was graciously forgiven, and this realization thrilled his soul. He had gladness in his heart, peace in his mind, and restful sleep throughout his nights. His writings reveal the peace of a contented soul. He did not lie awake at night worrying about what might have been. The God who held the universe held him. He was safe.

Christians should never be tormented by troublesome memories. John said, "If we confess our sins, he is faithful and just to forgive us our sins, and to cleanse us from all unrighteousness" (1 John 1:9). And in the same chapter he wrote, "And these things write we unto you, that your joy may be full" (1 John 1:4). It is impossible for a Christian to be filled with gladness when he is haunted by memories of former indiscretions. In Horatio Spafford's well-known words:

> My sin—O the bliss of this glorious thought—
> My sin, not in part, but the whole,
> Is nailed to His Cross, and I bear it no more:
> Praise the Lord, praise the Lord, O my soul!

WHEN YOU FEEL LIKE QUITTING, REMEMBER
PAUL, DEMAS, AND REVELATION 2:10

"Be thou faithful unto death, and I will give thee a crown of life."

This is an age of "drop-outs," that has brought nothing new to our world. Viewers of television programs are accustomed to commercials that warn students against dropping out of school, stating that better jobs and brighter futures await graduates from institutions of learning. The Bible also warns people against similar dangers that await those who forget and forsake their religious commitments. Initial enthusiasm for Christ and His kingdom is of little value if a person forsakes the cause he or she once championed. If the Christian life is compared with a race, then the athlete must remember the finish line is not *halfway* down the course. A runner who desires a trophy must continue—to the end!

Paul probably considered these facts when, sitting in his prison at Rome, he thought of his former companion, Demas. Regretfully, the apostle wrote to Timothy, saying, "Demas hath forsaken me, having loved this present world" (2 Tim. 4:10). It is not known what became of the young backslider, but there is reason to believe that later he wished he had been a wiser man. It is challenging to read the words of the Lord spoken to the church at Smyrna, "Be thou faithful unto death, and I will give thee a crown of life" (Rev. 2:10). The Christian experience may be summarized under three words: commencing, continuing, and conquering. Unless the first is followed by the second, something precious is lost.

Evidently Paul's young companion had made a commitment to Christ; otherwise he would not have been with the apostle in Rome. His subsequent experience may be considered under four words: his delight, distraction, departure, and disappearance. Paul had some knowledge of each of these phases in the life of his young helper. Did Demas quit because of the difficult circumstances that surrounded him? Was he disappointed and disillusioned when things continued to deteriorate? Was he afraid of the future, or fascinated by the night life of Rome? When Demas forsook Paul, he walked into eternal obscurity. If he lived to be an old man, he was probably dismayed with his memories. He lost his contentment and his crown and became a drop-out from the greatest enterprise in the world.

Perhaps Paul was thinking of this when he wrote, "I have fought a good fight, I have finished my course, I have kept the faith. Henceforth there is laid up for me a crown" (2 Tim. 4:7–8). The apostle made mistakes, but from the day he met the Lord outside of Damascus until he met Him again in heaven, Paul never faltered. Maybe he would have appreciated the moral of the little poem:

> Two frogs fell into a deep cream bowl;
> One was an optimistic soul,
> But the other took the gloomy view,
> "We shall drown!" he cried without adieu.
> So with a last despairing cry,
> He flung up his legs and said, "Goodbye!"
> Quote the other frog with a merry grin,
> "I can't get out, but I won't give in;
> I'll swim around 'til my strength is spent,
> Then will I die the more content."
> Bravely he swam 'til it would seem
> His struggles began to churn the cream.
> On the top of the butter at last he stopped,
> And out of the bowl he gaily hopped.
> What is the moral? It's easily found,
> If you can't hop out, keep swimming around!
>
> Author Unknown

If diamonds could speak they might complain of harsh treatment received during their preparation to become finished gems. There is a great difference between the stone found in the mines and the jewel of exquisited beauty placed in a royal crown. There is an even greater difference between the rough, unlovely sinner, and the finished product mentioned by John. The apostle wrote, "Beloved, now are we the sons of God, and it doth not yet appear what we shall be: but we know that, when he shall appear, we shall be like him; for we shall see him as he is" (1 John 3:2). If a diamond had the capability of dismissing its polisher, it would ruin the best plans ever conceived. That is true of any Christian who quits in the midst of God's redeeming operation. The Bible says, "Be ye stedfast, unmoveable, always abounding in the work of the Lord" (1 Cor. 15:58). *Never give up!*

WHEN YOU FEEL LIKE YOUR SHIP
IS SINKING, REMEMBER ACTS 27:24

*"Fear not, Paul; thou must be brought before Caesar: and,
lo, God hath given thee all them that sail with thee."*

During the early months of 1941, my wife and I were traveling in
the upper part of the Amazon River. One day, with other tourists, we
visited an Indian village. When we left the elegant cruise ship to step
into the jungle, we entered another world! Some of the local people
were very primitive. Their huts were crude, and the forests reached
the water's edge. The arrival of such a large ship had caused great
excitement. It provided the local people with the opportunity to sell
their curios. Two of our party saw a homemade boat, and wanted to
have their photograph taken sitting in it. They gave their camera to
another visitor and asked if he would take their picture. All the people
standing near were intent on watching the operation as he said, "Smile,"
but no one noticed the boat was sinking. Within minutes my friends
were sitting in the Amazon River. Everybody laughed except the pair
in the boat whose enthusiasm had been dampened!

Paul had a similar experience, but for him the event was not a
cause for humor. It was terrifying. His ship had been battered by a
great storm, and his prayers had apparently been in vain. The prospect of an early death was very real. Luke, the physician traveling
with the apostle, wrote, "And we being exceedingly tossed with a
tempest, the next day they lightened the ship. And the third day we
cast out with our own hands the tackling of the ship. And when
neither sun nor stars in many days appeared, and no small tempest
lay on us, all hope that we should be saved was then taken away"
(Acts 27:18–20).

Amid such frightening circumstances, Paul's attitude shone like
a beam from a lighthouse. For all who fear their ship is sinking,
Luke's account offers help.

An Unfinished Task

God said, "Fear not, thou must be brought before Caesar." As
long as a man's life is in alignment with the will of God, it is
impossible for him to die until God takes him. If his ship sinks, he
can only fall into the everlasting arms of God's tenderness. Many
people live as prodigals and only remember God in times of acute
adversity. It was not desperation that encouraged Paul to pray. It

was total dependence upon his Heavenly Father. His perfect love for the Lord cast out the fear of imminent death.

An Unwavering Trust

An elderly lady in the Highlands of Scotland said, "If you thatch your house in the summer, you need not fear the winter." There is a great difference between trust and terror. When confronted by the same storm, the other passengers on Paul's ship became desperately afraid. They had no idea what needed to be done and no Savior from whom to seek help. On the contrary, Paul spent time in the presence of God. He who often visits the mercy seat can find the way there even in the dark! The apostle knew circumstances could never change the compassion of God. Paul believed the Lord held the oceans in His hand. If God permitted the ship to sink, He could make even that catastrophe provide for the welfare of His children.

An Unexpected Thought

The apostle said to his companions, "Howbeit we must be cast upon a certain island" (Acts 27:26). He discovered that even in the midst of the terrible storm, God was fulfilling His purpose. The entire tempest was only a part of a greater plan to reach people with the Gospel. As far as Paul was concerned all things were ordered by the Almighty, and since He was directing the operation, the future of the sailors was assured. He did not see the threatening cloud but rather the silver edges around it—sure evidence the sun was still shining.

An Unmistakable Triumph

When Paul said to his shipmates, "Wherefore, sirs, be of good cheer, for I believe God, that it shall be even as it was told me," he exhibited unlimited faith (Acts 27:25). This explains the remarkable effect upon his companions. "Then were they all of good cheer" (Acts 27:36).

> Ye fearful saints, fresh courage take;
> The clouds ye so much dread
> Are big with mercy and will break
> In blessing on your heart.

WHEN YOUR SPIRITUAL ENTHUSIASM
IS WANING, REMEMBER PSALM 39:3

"While I was musing the fire burned."

Solomon was a king to whom God gave great wisdom. He asked, "Can a man take fire in his bosom, and his clothes not be burned?" (Prov. 6:27). His question was most likely based on personal experience. When he considered the worship of God, fires of devotion burned within his soul, and his outward appearance reflected the glory of God. When he considered the carnal pleasures of self-indulgence, his ideas led to illicit associations with foreign women, and lust destroyed his soul. Modern techniques fight fire with fire. Firemen deliberately light fires ahead of the main blaze so that the dry bush will not supply fuel for the approaching inferno.

Illicit thoughts within the mind, if unchecked, lead to destruction. The only effective preventative is to kindle holy fires which remove potential hazards. David apparently knew this also for he wrote, "While I was musing the fire burned." When his mind was filled with thoughts of God, his soul was delivered from temptation. Perhaps Paul expressed the same truth when he urged the Christians in Ephesus to wear "a helmet of salvation" (Eph. 6:17).

David . . . *Who Compromised*

"And it came to pass in an eveningtide, that David arose from off his bed, and walked upon the roof of the king's house: and . . . saw a woman washing herself; and the woman was very beautiful to look upon. And David sent and inquired after the woman" (2 Sam. 11:2–3). The night was still and serene, but the king's heart was pounding! The day had been hot and stifling, and vainly seeking rest, David had lain upon his bed. The afternoon seemed endless, but when the evening breezes offered respite from the oppressive conditions, the king walked on the roof of his palace.

Suddenly, he saw a very beautiful lady, and his heart seemed to miss a beat. Within the seclusion of her protected garden, Bathsheba was bathing, She also had suffered from the distressing heat of that eastern day. Believing herself safe from the attention of neighbors, the woman washed her perspiring body, completely unaware of David's watchful eyes. She could not have known at that moment the evil kindling a fire in the king's heart. Had he extinguished the initial spark, an inferno would have been prevented.

Saul . . . *Who Collapsed*

He was mad and determined! Saul was convinced the Christians were undermining the faith of the fathers, and their irresponsibility had to be checked. While "he mused on these things, the fire burned within him."

"And Saul, yet breathing out threatenings and slaughter against the disciples of the Lord, went unto the high priest, and desired of him letters to Damascus to the synagogues, that if he found any of this way, whether they were men or women, he might bring them bound unto Jerusalem" (Acts 9:1–2). It was said of this man that "he made havock of the church" (Acts 8:3).

The word translated "havoc" is *elumaineto* which was often used to describe the work of a wild pig, whose snout literally tore up young plants in a vineyard. Saul of Tarsus, driven mercilessly by a troubled conscience, resembled an animal destroying God's garden. Relentlessly he went from house to house seeking Christians whom he threw into prison. Who would have thought that during this onslaught on the church, God was watching, waiting, and perhaps smiling? Saul was a large fish which the Spirit of God had hooked.

Knowing that something strange was happening, Saul resisted fiercely. He would never surrender! He would fight to the end. Yet God was holding the line, and the end was never in doubt (from the author's commentary, *The Amazing Acts*, page 117. Published by Kregel Publications, Grand Rapids, Michigan). God was lighting another fire to extinguish the first.

Stephen . . . *Who Conquered*

Stephen supplied the greatest example of this attractive truth. It has been said that prevention is better than any cure. There were numerous reasons why Stephen might have been filled with animosity, jealousy and frustration. He was one of the greatest preachers in the early church but was relegated to delivering aid to complaining widows. He might have been one of the greatest evangelists but became the first martyr.

He could have detested his persecutors but instead prayed for their forgiveness. It seems the only fire within his soul was kindled by God. While Stephen mused, the fire burned, and in its glow, he saw "the glory of God, and Jesus standing on the right hand of God" (Acts 7:55). When your spiritual enthusiasm is waning—stop, *think*, and kindle a fire of spiritual passion!

25

"Love your enemies, bless them that curse you, do good to them that hate you, and pray for them which despitefully use you, and persecute you."

The Savior commanded His followers to love their enemies, but that, in all probability, was their most difficult assignment. Some people profess to love everybody, but evade the real issue by admitting they do not *like* everybody! When an innocent person has been maliciously slandered, and his influence for Christ and the church ruined, it becomes increasingly difficult to ignore what has been done. The idea of turning the other cheek is not the most popular Christian teaching. The Bible supplies notable examples of people who succeeded in overlooking the faults of their enemies.

David . . . *Who Spared the Life of King Saul*

The story of Saul's inexcusable jealousy of the lad from Bethlehem has become one of the most infamous accounts in literature. Although David had given great service to his master, his kindly attitude was completely ignored, and a quivering lance embedded in the wall of the palace gave eloquent evidence of the monarch's ill temper. When David was given the opportunity to remove his enemy forever, everybody was amazed by the kindness of the long-suffering fugitive. His refusal to kill the tyrant guaranteed he would be worthy to reign over Israel (see 1 Sam. 26:6–9).

Martha . . . *Who Never Complained Again*

Martha was very flustered. She was expecting about twenty guests for dinner, and she wanted everything to be perfect. Jesus and his twelve disciples would be present, probably Simon the leper, one of her neighbors would attend, and a few extra friends would spend the evening with them. Of course it would mean extra work and careful planning, but Mary would be a great help in arranging the details. But where was she?

Then Martha's eyes seemed to grow larger, and her blood pressure began to rise. It could not be! Her sister would never ignore her responsibilities in the kitchen! Martha glanced into the living room and rebelled. "Now it came to pass, as they went, that he entered into a certain village: and a certain woman named Martha received him into her house. And she had a sister called Mary, which also sat at Jesus' feet, and heard his word. But Martha was cumbered about much serving, and came to him, and said, Lord, dost thou not care that my sister hath left me to serve alone? bid her therefore that she help me" (Luke 10:38–40).

It must be admitted that Martha had legitimate reasons for complaint, but there is no record that she ever complained again. Other women might have sulked through the evening, and then refused to speak to the thoughtless sister for the rest of the week. Martha had not only invited Jesus into her home, but she welcomed Him into her heart.

The Savior . . . *Who Spoke of an Unforgiving Servant*

The Lord Jesus, who never carried a grudge against anybody, told a remarkable story of an unforgiving man. He intimated in His parable that a king's honored servant embezzled a large sum of money which was assessed at 10,000 talents. Today that would be in excess of two hundred million dollars. When the criminal confessed his sin and asked for pardon, his master forgave him. Yet, the same man refused to pardon a fellow servant who only owed seven dollars and fifty cents.

"And his lord was wroth, and delivered him to the tormentors, till he should pay all that was due unto him." The Savior continued, "So likewise shall my heavenly Father do also unto you, if ye from your hearts forgive not every one his brother their trespasses" (see Matt. 18:23–35).

These were solemn words which we may or may not appreciate. Yet one thing became obvious: if people expect to be forgiven by God, they must be willing to exhibit the same kindness in their associations with other people. Forgiveness is a seed capable of producing a great harvest.

When I was a young preacher, I spent five years preaching in Great Britain. I met and heard many other evangelists, but none impressed me so much as did the workers in the Salvation Army. For example, I heard of a young Salvationist called Jenny. One night as she spoke to her audience, a drunken man at the back of the crowd threw a potato which struck her in the face. For a few moments she seemed disconcerted, but quickly recovering, continued to preach the Gospel. Later that evening she planted the potato in her garden and at the next Harvest Thanksgiving Service proudly displayed a basket of attractive golden potatoes. Then she took them to an old pensioner, and her gift supplied food for a whole week. God is able to make even the wrath of men to praise Him (see Ps. 76:10). He can do even more when His people cooperate with Him (see Col. 3:13).

WHEN YOU THINK YOU CAN'T,
REMEMBER PHILIPPIANS 4:13

*"I can do all things through Christ
which strengtheneth me."*

I knew a lady who was an excellent game player, but she was her own worst enemy. Fully convinced of her inability to compete successfully, she would systematically explain reasons for her incompetence. Having done this, she would surprise herself with excellent play which vanquished her opponents. She would say, "I cannot do it," but she was mistaken.

It has often been claimed that it is better to try and fail than never to try. Francis Gay, in *The Friendship Book for 1972*, quoted these lines from an unknown author:

> If you think you're beaten, you are. If you think you dare not,
>   you don't.
> If you'd like to win, but you think you can't, it's almost certain,
>   you won't.
> If you think you'll lose, you've lost, for out in the world, you'll find
> That success begins in a fellow's will—it's all in the state
>   of the mind.
> Think big, and your deeds will grow. Think small, and you'll
>   fall behind.
> Think you can win, and you will—it's all in the state of mind.
> Life's battles often go to the stronger or faster man.
> But sooner or later, the man who wins is the man who thinks he can.

Consider Goliath Who Said He Would and Couldn't

He was a one–man mountain, the pride of all Philistia, and the hero of the nation's army. When the sun shone upon his glistening armor, it was easy to believe the mountain was being set on fire. When he roared his challenge to Israel, it sounded like thunder preceding a storm. When he flexed his muscles and waved his enormous weapons, his opponents trembled. Yet the giant was amazed when a small boy with pebbles in his hand challenged his superiority. This was an affront to his dignity, an unforgivable insult to his prowess.

"And the Philistine said to David, Come to me, and I will give thy flesh unto the fowls of the air, and to the beasts of the field" (1 Sam. 17:44).

His face was flushed with fury—tis child was not even a dog, he was a senseless puppy! "Then said David to the Philistine, Thou comest to me with a sword, and with a spear, and with a shield, but I come to thee in the name of the LORD of hosts, the God of the armies of Israel whom thou hast defied. This day will the LORD deliver thee into mine hand . . . that all the earth may know that there is a God in Israel" (1 Sam. 17:45–46).

That small boy was tall enough to look over the shoulder of the giant and see God behind him. Goliath said, "I will" but couldn't. David said, "I will" and did!

Consider Philip Who Said He Couldn't and Did

The Sea of Galilee was probably resplendent with the glow of a setting sun. The evening breeze was gently playing a tune in the leaves of the trees. As Jesus looked from the hill to see the immense multitude that had followed him, He sighed. They were hungry. They were "as sheep without a shepherd." The children were asking for food, but the excited parents were too intent on waiting for another miracle to pay attention to the needs of their offspring. It was wonderful to tell people about the bread of life, but they needed a meal. The little people had to be fed.

"[Jesus] saith unto Philip, Whence shall we buy bread, that these may eat? And this he said to prove him: for he himself knew what he would do. Philip answered him, Two hundred pennyworth of bread is not sufficient for them, that every one of them may take a little" (John 6:5–7).

Master, what you suggest is impossible. I would need to work every day for nine months in order to obtain enough money to buy provisions for this crowd. There are no shops, and we have no money. A boy's lunch! Five barley loaves and a couple of small fish! Pardon my laughter, Lord, but common sense says it can't be done.

And yet it was done, and Philip helped do it. What a difference Jesus made in that difficult situation. It is not known whether Philip ever met the apostle Paul, but in any case, he would have fully agreed with Paul's statement, "I can do all things through Christ which strengtheneth me."

Consider Paul Who Said He Could and Did

Paul was an enigma, difficult to understand and even harder to explain. Writing to the Corinthians he said, "Of the Jews five times

30

received I forty stripes save one." Therefore on five different occasions he was lashed for his faith—but he could not be silenced! "Thrice was I beaten with rods, once was I stoned." Other prisoners died during such punishment, but Paul survived. "Thrice I suffered shipwreck, a night and a day I have been in the deep." He either clung to the wreckage of a ship, or lay in a tossing lifeboat, yet he did not sink (see 2 Cor. 11:24–33). It is believed that Paul suffered from extremely poor eyesight, yet his letters comprise most of the New Testament. He could not have been a robust man, yet within his lifetime he evangelized the known world. He did not always succeed in his mission, but he never quit. Men and women of his caliber never do.

WHEN THE PRESSURES OF LIFE MAKE YOU IRRITABLE, REMEMBER ISAIAH 30:15 AND MARK 6:31

"For thus saith the Lord GOD, the Holy One of Israel . . . in quietness and in confidence shall be your strength." "Come ye yourselves apart into a desert place, and rest a while."

When the children of Israel entered Canaan, they were given explicit instructions regarding their agriculture. "When ye come into the land which I give you, then shall the land keep a sabbath unto the LORD. Six years thou shalt sow thy field, and six years thou shalt prune thy vineyard, and gather the fruit thereof. But in the seventh year shall be a sabbath of rest unto the land, a sabbath for the LORD: thou shalt neither sow thy field, nor prune thy vineyard" (Lev. 25:2–4).

During the passing of time, regulations changed the attitude of farmers. Aware of the increasing needs of mankind, governments ordered that fertilizers and other commodities be used to restore the elements removed by successive crops. Fields are not "rested" as they once were.

When a man or woman works under pressure, irritability is inevitable. When people are emotionally upset, they say and do things which beget tension and destructiveness. Relationships are ruined, and contacts with neighbors become a nightmare. God knew this and prepared a remedy for His people.

Stillness . . . *The Mother of Confidence*

During my stay in Rotorua, New Zealand, I went with a famous guide to see the wonders of the national park. All around were pools of boiling mud and geysers of varying size. Yet the main attraction was the huge central waterspout which sent a column of water high into the air. When it seemed reluctant to entertain visitors, I saw a slight frown appear on the face of the lady lecturer. Suddenly, she approached and threw something into the base of the geyser. Within moments the earth seemed to erupt, and the famous phenomenon came to life. I was fascinated when she explained, "Sometimes, it is necessary to throw some detergent into the gaping hole. I do not know what happens exactly, but the trick always works."

I smiled, for I had often seen the same phenomenon among men and women. Volcanic eruptions are not reserved exclusively for national parks. Sometimes eruptive energy fills the souls of human

32

beings, and it only needs a little encouragement. One unwise word or thoughtless action may lead to problems in a home, a community, and even among nations. Such energy needs to be quelled, not encouraged! Jesus said to His exultant followers, "Come apart, and rest awhile," and to make this possible, He led the disciples into the desert. They needed to be still and know that He was God.

Solitude . . . *The Means of Communion*

Many teachers believe that Moses did not deserve the punishment which terminated his ministry. He had brought Israel out from the bondage of Egypt to the borders of Canaan. That he should be excluded from Canaan because of the failure of the people and his own moment of anger when he smote the rock seemed to be a travesty of justice. God had special reasons for His treatment of Israel's leader, but it is thought-provoking that during his times of testing Moses climbed into the mountain where his ruffled spirit was calmed.

> "To bear up under loss; to fight the bitterness of defeat, and the weakness of grief; to be victor over anger; to smile when tears are close; to resist evil men and base instincts; to hate hate, and love love; to go on when it would seem good to die; to seek after the glory and the dream; to look up with unquenchable faith . . . that is what any man can do, and so be great." —Zane Grey

Self-Restraint . . . *The Method of Conquest*

Moses and Paul belonged to the same family. In some ways they might have been twins! Paul gave his life for people who criticized him, and he sacrificed everything that undeserving people might be helped. Surely there were occasions when his natural instincts desired to retaliate, but on the solitary occasion when he yielded to impulse, he apologized for his outburst (see Acts 23:1–5). His phenomenal success was due, at least in part, to the steady hold he maintained upon his personal feelings. He had learned to say, "Not I, but Christ liveth in me" (Gal. 2:20).

Too much work can promote oppression, worry, discontent, and, finally, criticism of other people. Since the tongue can be a dangerous member of the body, it is often wise to keep one's mouth closed!

God said, "In quietness and confidence shall be your strength," and this is an excellent text for a depressed or irritable soul.

*"And it came to pass, as she continued praying before the LORD,
that Eli marked her mouth. Now Hannah, she spake in her heart;
only her lips moved, but her voice was not heard: therefore Eli
thought she had been drunken. And Eli said unto her, How
long wilt thou be drunken? Put away thy wine from thee."*

It is a terrible thing to be misjudged and condemned, especially
when the criticism comes from a person who should know better.
During moments of anguish the soul may become hurt, annoyed
and retaliatory—or miraculously tolerant and patient. Let it be
admitted, it is difficult to remain serene when unkind words undermine one's influence for God. The Bible supplies numerous
examples of people who remained calm under fire.

Hannah Who Interceded

The woman was desperate. She had no child, and according to the
belief of her culture, her barrenness was considered to be a curse
from God. To make matters worse, her husband's second wife "provoked her sore, for to make her fret, because the LORD had shut up
her womb" (1 Sam. 1:6–7).

Hannah was filled with sadness when she prayed silently before the altar
at Shiloh. "She spake in her heart; only her lips moved, but her voice was
not heard; therefore Eli thought she had been drunken." The words spoken
by the high priest were humiliating, but Hannah remained calm. Had she
denounced the priest, she might have lost the greatest blessing of her life.

David Who Intervened

Poor David! He was perplexed. He was being accused of all
kinds of indiscretions and was being hunted as "a partridge in the
mountains" (1 Sam. 26:20). Then suddenly it seemed his troubles
were ending; Saul, who had misjudged and vilified him, lay at his
feet. "Then said Abishai to David, God hath delivered thine enemy into thine hand this day; now therefore let me smite him, I
pray thee, with the spear even to the earth at once, and I will not
smite him the second time. And David said to Abishai, Destroy
him not: for who can stretch forth his hand against the LORD's
anointed, and be guiltless?" (1 Sam. 26:8–9).

If David had acted impetuously, he would have made one of his greatest mistakes. He subdued his anger, and any desire for revenge or self-justification was suppressed. Perhaps he listened to God who said, "To me belongeth vengeance, and recompense" (Deut. 32:35).

The Savior Who Instructed

The Sermon on the Mount was the greatest message ever delivered to a congregation. The hillside audience was enthralled and yet amazed by the words of Jesus the Carpenter. His ideas were different from anything they had ever heard. His highways to blessing ran through unexplored territory. The people had been taught to resist enemies, and in a corrupt world they knew how to survive. Jesus introduced a new life-style, and they were not sure whether they could accept it.

They listened as the Teacher said, "Blessed are ye when men shall revile you, and persecute you, and shall say all manner of evil against you falsely, for my sake. Rejoice, and be exceeding glad: for great is your reward in heaven" (Matt. 5:11–12).

The Lord not only recommended these virtues, He practiced what He preached. Of Him it was said, "Who, when he was reviled, reviled not again; when he suffered, he threatened not: but committed himself to him that judgeth righteously" (1 Peter 2:23). It should never be forgotten that when God raised the Lord and exalted him to the right hand of the Majesty on high, the Savior had more than demonstrated His worthiness for that honor. His amazing teaching must be the inspiration of the church, and His deeds the example for every Christian.

Paul Who Imitated

The church at Corinth was composed of a cosmopolitan people who did not live together peacefully. Although Paul founded and established the church, he was not always proud of his converts. His message to them was self-explanatory. "Being reviled, we bless; being persecuted, we suffer it: Being defamed, we intreat; we are made as the filth of the world, and are the offscouring of all things unto this day. I write not these things to shame you, but as my beloved sons I warn you. For though ye have ten thousand instructers in Christ, yet have ye not many fathers; for in Christ Jesus I have begotten you through the gospel. Wherefore, I beseech you, be ye followers of me" (1 Cor. 4:12–16).

Paul's advice was obvious. When Christians are attacked by unkind critics, they should ascertain if there was truth in the statements; if not, they should rejoice. Their attitude would guarantee excellent company.

35

WHEN YOUR BODY SEEMS TO BE FALLING APART, REMEMBER PHILIPPIANS 3:21

"[The Lord] shall change our vile body, that it may be fashioned like unto his glorious body, according to the working whereby he is able even to subdue all things unto himself."

Mrs. Scott was a charming lady whose children attended my Sunday School. She only came to my services on rare occasions for she was very heavy and very sensitive about her appearance. Diets and reducing exercises were of no value because of her other ailments. One day as I sat beside her bed, she said, "Tell me about the new body I shall receive in heaven."

Momentarily, I was speechless, but she continued, "See, Pastor, my feet are already dead. Gangrene has set in and is spreading up my legs. I have not long to live and would like to know something about the new body I shall receive when this one has been forgotten." Her eyes were bright, and her face was radiant as she waited for my answer. My emotions were stirred, but just then her daughter entered the room and said, "Mother, the insurance man is at the door; he wants his money."

My sick friend said, "Oh, tell him to come back next week. I am about to hear about my new body." The daughter was very surprised, but I couldn't repress laughter. I was about to instruct a lady who could exclaim triumphantly, "O death, where is thy sting? O grave, where is thy victor?" (1 Cor. 15:55).

His Glorious Body . . . *It Was Real*

The Bible says that when the disciples thought they had seen a spirit, He said unto them, "Why are ye troubled? and why do thoughts arise in your hearts? Behold my hands and my feet, that it is I myself: handle me, and see; for a spirit hath not flesh and bones, as ye see me have" (Luke 24:38–39).

The church has always been troubled by heretics who said the Lord's resurrection was not physical, that He only rose in spirit, that His body remained in the grave and ultimately decayed and became dust. That view is not only wrong; it is insulting. It implies that Christ was a liar. When the disciples thought they were being visited by a ghost or spirit, Jesus instantly reminded them they were looking at flesh and bones. When they remained unconvinced, He asked for food and shared their meal. There was nothing phony about His appearances. His body was real, and Mrs. Scott was thrilled as I explained these facts.

His Glorious Body . . . *It Was Remarkable*

Jesus was in some respects limited during His ministry. If He had cast Himself from the pinnacle of the temple, His body would have been injured on the rocks. Throughout the storm on the sea of Galilee, the Lord was overcome by weariness and slept in the boat. If the Savior arrived unexpectedly at a home, He was obliged to announce His presence by knocking. Yet after His resurrection a closed door was unable to prevent His entry into the room where the disciples were gathered (see John 20:26). When Christ ascended from the mount of Olives, His body resisted the laws of gravity, and the watching disciples saw His entry into the clouds. His mortal body had put on immortality. He had been changed and glorified. I told Mrs. Scott that she would have a body exactly like His. Suffering and pain, and all kinds of physical problems would belong to the past. Even elderly people would become young again.

His Glorious Body . . . *It Was Recognizable*

It is probable that the Lord had the power to disguise Himself! Mark described this as "another form" (Mark 16:12). When Mary came to the sepulcher, she saw someone she assumed was the gardener. Maybe she was blinded by her tears or too preoccupied to look closely at the Man standing near the tomb. Yet within moments she was able to say, "Rabboni!" (John 20:16).

Thomas was the greatest doubter of the disciples, but he recognized the Lord when he cried, "My Lord, and my God" (John 20:28). Charles Haddon Spurgeon was asked by a lady in his church, "Shall we know each other in heaven?" The pastor's reply was abrupt and challenging. He said, "Do you think we shall be bigger fools up there than we are down here?" My ailing sister in the Lord smiled. What I said made sense!

The pains of old age increase steadily, and every one threatens to become fatal! Recently I telephoned a friend to ask how she was recovering from an illness. She said, "I don't know what to say, except that my old body seems to be falling apart." Thank God, a new body awaits every Christian; it will last forever. Funeral directors, doctors, and hospital facilities will be unknown in eternity.

WHEN YOU CAN'T SLEEP, REMEMBER SAMUEL WHO HAD A SIMILAR EXPERIENCE. 1 SAMUEL 3:10

"And the Lord came, and stood, and called as at other times, Samuel, Samuel. Then Samuel answered, Speak; for thy servant heareth."

David believed God gave sleep to His people (see Ps. 127:2), but there are occasions when his faith might have been challenged. Sleep was designed by God to bring rest to weary bodies and refreshment to tired minds. Nevertheless, sometimes sleep is elusive. Overwhelming noise, over-active minds, overpowering pain, and sometimes, over-filled stomachs prevent people from obtaining necessary rest. Consequently, the manufacturers and dispensers of sleeping pills are making their fortunes. It might be wise to consider that occasionally even the Lord disturbs His slumbering people.

When Jonah was awakened on his run-away voyage to Tarshish, the captain of the vessel said to him, "What meanest thou, O sleeper? arise, call upon thy God, if so be that God will think upon us, that we perish not" (Jonah 1:6). The shipmaster's timely intervention changed Jonah's attitude and saved the lives of his crew. When Ahasuerus, the king of Babylon was unable to sleep, he was used by God to prevent the death of Mordecai and save the lives of many Hebrews (see Esther 6:1). Quite recently a friend said to me, "I do not sleep much these nights, so I use the time to pray for you." Repeatedly, Paul said that he prayed for his friends night and day (see 1 Thess. 3:10 and 2 Tim. 1:3). Perhaps some of God's people are so preoccupied during the day that they need to make up for lost time at night! It is better to pray than to remain restless in bed.

A young lady once said to me, "I do most of my praying at night, and the Devil hates it! He does not like my praying so much, and quickly puts me to sleep. Praying works better than sleeping pills!" When the boy named Samuel was unable to sleep, he discovered God was calling him to great service. When he listened, the Lord revealed facts unknown to other people. Quite recently I awakened in the middle of the night, and I asked as I lay in bed, "Why did God permit this to happen? It must be because I need to pray for someone." Instantly, the name of a Christian brother came into my mind. I spent the next few minutes asking God to help that man. I know now that he had a great need. Furthermore, after my prayers had been uttered, I slept for the rest of the night.

During our visit to South Africa, my wife and I stayed for a time in a missionary home. We met a charming missionary who was also a temporary guest. One day I asked about her most exciting experience on the mission field. She described how her first real assignment was to accompany an older missionary on a special trek to reach a certain tribe of cannibals. When they arrived they discovered the chief did not want white people in his district. He probably feared he would be reported for some of the practices he encouraged. He grumbled, and pointing to a mud hut and said, "You can stay there tonight, but tomorrow you leave."

Mrs Phipson paused, and it was easy to see she was reliving her experience in that hostile village. She continued, "I was wide awake, and while my partner slept, I listened to noises outside the hut. Finally, I crawled to the small door and saw we were surrounded by natives who were flat on their stomachs, wriggling like worms toward us. I hurried to awaken my senior worker who, realizing our danger, said, 'Quick, light the lamp. Let them see that we are awake.' Then we made tea and drank it. Then we made more tea and drank that! We continued until dawn. During this time the head-hunters finally left us."

I was about to interrupt with a question when she lifted her hand and said, "I have not finished. The next morning we left, and to be honest I was glad to get away. Three weeks later a native runner from the base station overtook us with our mail. My friend opened one of her letters to discover a lady overseas had written to ask, 'Did you have any special need on (and the date was given). I could not sleep that night for your face haunted me. I turned over and over in my bed, but had no rest until I prayed specially for you. Suddenly, I knew everything was alright, but I would like to know what happened on that particular night.'" Mrs. Phipson said, "I kept a diary in those days, so I was able to turn its pages to answer her question. On the night that lady was constrained to pray for her friend—that was the night the cannibals left us." It pays to pray—even when you cannot sleep.

"For ye have need of patience. . . . For yet a little while,
and he that shall come will come, and will not tarry."

I was very desperate, but in my own defense let me add I was also inexperienced and had much to learn. I expected God to turn the world upside down, but it seemed I was more concerned than He. My services had continued nightly for three weeks. The large Gospel Hall was crowded to capacity, but no one had responded to my invitation to trust the Savior. At that time I was twenty years old, and my enthusiasm exceeded my knowledge! The local Christians appeared to be disappointed, and I thought they were beginning to blame me for the lack of visible results in the meetings. My hostess was a dynamic lady whose love for the Lord overflowed. Night after night she stared at me and said, "There is a difference between praying, and praying through." Each time she repeated the statement, I felt that somewhere I had failed. Actually, I began to resent her words and wanted to say, "Then why don't you pray through and get things moving?" I was afraid to challenge her, however, and remained silent!

I prayed by the hour but the meetings became progressively worse. I was so certain God would answer my appeal for help that one night I said to the congregation, "After we have prayed, I shall go to the counseling room to wait for you. I have asked the Lord to bring six souls to Himself." But when everybody went away, I felt horribly alone and became resentful. I knelt by a chair and said, "Lord, it's not fair. I'm doing all the work down here, and You are doing nothing!" That was a very stupid thing to say, but, as I have already explained, I was desperate. Then suddenly I heard a voice saying, "If I could save souls as easily as you think I can, I would have saved the whole world long ago."

That dynamic utterance destroyed my ego and left me in a state of confusion. I had never known an experience when God's voice was so authoritative and real. Nevertheless, my disturbed and disappointed soul was still rebellious. I placed my Bible on the chair before me, closed my eyes, stabbed with my finger at the unseen page, and said, "Alright, Lord, if You cannot save all these people, at least say something to me." When I opened my eyes to see the verse at which my finger pointed, I read, "For ye have need of

40

patience that, after ye have done the will of God, ye might receive the promise. For yet a little while, and he that shall come will come, and will not tarry." I was astounded. I had neither heard nor read that text and was unaware it was in the Bible.

Later that night I climbed into my bed, pulled the blankets over my head, and prayed until I fell asleep. The next afternoon when I entered the sanctuary, I took one step down the aisle and suddenly stopped. I knew something had happened. The entire building seemed to be filled with the presence of God. Perhaps the change had taken place within me, but everything appeared to be different. The service which followed had been especially convened for Christians; I neither preached the Gospel nor issued an invitation, and yet amazing things happened.

A soldier about to leave said, "Sir, I am the boxing champion of my regiment." I looked at his flattened nose, smiled, and said, "Fellow, there was at least one punch you didn't dodge." He grinned and replied, "Yes, sir, I knocked out a lot of fighters, but today the love of God has knocked me out." He came to the front of the sanctuary with three other soldiers, and they were the first of about seventy adults who came to know Christ as their Savior. They were the firstfruits of a wonderful harvest. Since that day I have never complained of a difficult assignment or the lack of converts in my evangelistic crusades. I really did have need of patience, for He who intended to come did come to that Gospel Hall at Lerwick in the Shetland Islands.

The person who wrote the epistle to the Hebrews was aware of the tremendous trials besetting the church of his day. The Roman Empire was attempting to annihilate Christians. The faith of new believers was being challenged. The temple at Jerusalem was either destroyed or was about to be destroyed. Many believers were being fed to ravenous beasts or burned to death in the emperor's garden. To many of these suffering people it must have seemed a waste of time to pray. Whatever they requested, it appeared God was either indifferent to the needs of His people or not sufficiently interested to listen to their desperate requests. Yet the writer of this remarkable letter stood firm in the midst of the storm, and his words echoed amazing confidence. He was sure the Lord would come, and he was not mistaken.

"When he (Jesus) had heard therefore that he (Lazarus) was
sick, he abode two days still in the same place where he was."

The home in Bethany was strangely silent. Lazarus was dead, and his sisters were devastated. The laughter known during the visits of Jesus had disappeared. Martha, who was an excellent cook, had no desire to remain in her kitchen. Everything had changed. She and her sister had nursed their ailing brother and toward the end of his illness sent an urgent appeal for assistance to Jesus.

Alas! They now believed their request had fallen upon deaf ears. Their Friend was not interested. He had remained two days doing things which could have been postponed! Now it was too late to do anything. Their brother had been buried, and life in the home seemed meaningless. It was difficult to decide which was worse—that Lazarus had died or that Jesus had let them down. Their outlook was intensely bleak, and probably Martha and Mary would have disagreed if someone suggested the sun would shine again.

Let us not blame them. They had watched the sufferings of their brother and had prayed earnestly that God would spare him. Their prayers had remained unanswered, and apparently even Jesus did not care. Such circumstances challenge the faith of even the greatest Christians. Inevitably the question arose, "Why did God allow this to happen to us?" It should always be remembered that shadows are caused by light—there are no shadows in darkness. Even stars reflect the light of the sun, and although storms may temporarily hide it, *the sun is always shining.*

God's Profound Patience

When Mary and Martha believed the Lord had insufficient interest to respond to their desperate plea for help, He also was troubled. He could never forget His friends, but much more was at stake than the extension of a man's life. Good photographs are only developed in darkness. Jesus was waiting for gloom to envelop His dearest friends in order to produce within their souls His likeness. They were waiting for Him, and He was waiting for them.

God's Prepared Plan

When Jesus eventually arrived in Bethany, Martha went to meet him and said, "Lord, if thou hadst been here, my brother had not died. But I know, that even now, whatsoever thou wilt ask of God, God will give it thee" (John 11:21–22). The subsequent Scriptures reveal that her faith related to events of the last day. Jesus was more concerned that she understood the significance of what was to happen that day. His followers had recognized Him to be a wonderful Friend, a tremendous Teacher, and even a possible Messiah. None, however, believed Him to be God's Son. The raising of a dead man was nothing compared with opening their blind eyes.

Gods Prepared Place

Christ knew what He intended to do. Lazarus would soon be home again, but there was much more at stake than performing a miracle. Lazarus would eventually die again, and there would be no earthly healer to whom a message for help could be despatched. If people believed Him to be the Son of God, then just as easily as He brought Lazarus back to be with them in Bethany, He could also guarantee his presence in heaven. The happiness of those bereaved sisters did not depend on the immediate resurrection of their brother, but on their increasing understanding of the greatness of their Friend, Jesus of Nazareth. This truth was enunciated when a little later Jesus said to His disciples, "Let not your heart be troubled; ye believe in God, believe also in me . . . I go to prepare a place for you. And if I go and prepare a place for you, I will come again, and receive you unto myself; that where I am, there ye may be also" (John 14:1–3).

God's Perfect Peace

It is easy to hear the Lord saying, "Mary, if you are still alive when your brother dies again, do not grieve. Stand by his grave and say exultantly, 'O death, where is thy sting? O grave, where is thy victory?'" (1 Cor. 15:55). When the women understood His message, the sun was shining again! God's ways are not always our ways, but His ways are always best. If darkness surrounds you now, be of good cheer. It will pass!

WHEN YOU FEEL LONELY, REMEMBER OTHERS WHO FELT THE SAME WAY AND JOSHUA 1:5; 1 KINGS 19:10; ACTS 23:11

The feeling of loneliness can be a depressing experience. It is possible to feel lonely in a crowd, to see innumerable faces, none of which can be recognized. A few people choose to become hermits; others confine themselves to religious institutions believing that in solitude peace be found. Yet the fact remains that most people love the company of other human beings, and consequently, when circumstances isolate them, despondency is never far away. A boy away at school, a member of the armed services separated from family, a young missionary in a foreign land, and even travelers whose occupation demands sacrifice—all can be frustrated by loneliness. The Bible has a special message for such people.

The Man Who Was Lonely in a Crowd (Joshua 1:5)

Poor Joshua! When God said, "Moses my servant is dead," an ominous chill was felt throughout Israel, but no man was more affected than the new leader who was asked to succeed the revered patriarch. His task was unenviable for circumstances would often separate him from the most important people in the nation. Critics would shatter his tranquility, insurmountable obstacles would challenge his ingenuity, and a sense of inadequacy would undermine his confidence. Even the Lord recognized the weight of the burden to be carried, and with great wisdom said, "As I was with Moses so I will be with thee: I will not fail thee, nor forsake thee." Although many problems arose to confront and confuse Israel's leader, Joshua knew he could never be alone again. He welcomed solitude, for in the stillness, it was easier to hear the voice of his Master.

The Man Who Was Lonely in a Cave (1 Kings 19:10)

Poor Elijah! He who had been hunted by men was now haunted by memories. He had stood triumphantly before a multitude but had been frightened by a sinful woman. Jezebel had ruined his ministry and threatened to end his life. At the height of his career Elijah failed to do his duty, and as he hid in a mountain cave, probably wished he were dead. Had it been possible for Elijah and Jonah to meet, they could have talked long into the night. The reluctant messenger to Nineveh would have appreciated the feelings of his older brother. Jonah felt desperately alone when he said, "Therefore now, O LORD, take, I beseech thee, my life from me; for it is better for me to die, than to live" (Jonah 4:3).

When a healthy man loses the desire to live, it is generally because of failure and disappointment within his life. The person who continually thinks about disasters, disorders and defeats has no time to consider the promises of God. Elijah listened to the voices of nature and remained unmoved; when he was still, a whisper from the Lord stirred his soul and he realized he was not alone.

The Man Who Was Lonely in a Cell (Acts 23:11)

Poor Paul! Two years in a prison cell would be sufficient to sadden the heart of any man, but for Paul the time was heart-breaking. He had traversed continents and preached to multitudes of people. He sighed when he remembered those exhilarating meetings. But everything had changed, and Paul was desperately alone. He had few friends and preached only to his guards. His imprisonment had been occasioned by an intense desire to attend a festival at Jerusalem. God warned him to stay away from the feast but unfortunately the apostle's enthusiasm ran away with his reason! Luke's statement was self-explanatory: "And finding disciples, we tarried there seven days: who said to Paul through the Spirit, that he should not go up to Jerusalem" (Acts 21:4). Paul disregarded that command, and when it was too late to change his attitude, he was alone with accusing memories. The two years of incarceration might have been used proclaiming the Gospel of Christ.

Then a wonderful thing happened. "And the night following the Lord stood by him, and said, Be of good cheer, Paul: for as thou hast testified of me in Jerusalem, so must thou bear witness also at Rome" (Acts 23:11). Paul's disobedience did not indicate God had forsaken him. Much work still had to be accomplished. The prisoner's spirit was liberated even before his prison door opened. The Lord visited Joshua, Elijah and Paul.

Are you alone in a crowd, a cave, or a cell? Look carefully around. God is nearer than you can imagine.

"When my father and my mother forsake thee, then the Lᴏʀᴅ will take me up." "Can a woman forget her sucking child, that she should not have compassion on the son of her womb? yea, they may forget, yet will I not forget thee."

During a visit to Thailand, I met a teenager whose testimony thrilled my soul. He was selling ties to tourists and was doing a brisk trade. Crowded barges were bringing tourists to the Temple of the Dawn, and each visitor was a potential customer. My wife and I sat on a low wall watching his efforts when, suddenly, between the arrival of boats, he asked, "Sir, are you a Christian?" I assured him I was and asked if he also loved the Savior. Instantly he replied, "Yes, Sir, I gave my heart to Jesus two years ago." His smile disappeared as he continued, "That was when my father put me out of the home."

I was intrigued by his statement, and asked for more information. The boy said, "I attend an American mission, and our missionary told us that unless we witness for Jesus, people will remain in the dark. When I became a Christian, my father was very angry and said: 'I don't want you in my family.' So he turned me out, and I went to sleep in the doorway of an empty shop."

I said, "And now you are selling ties?"

"Yes, sir, and I am slowly saving my money because one day I hope to go to Bible school and learn how to become a missionary." At fourteen years of age he was expelled from his home only to discover he was falling into the everlasting arms of God's love.

David's text was not exactly a promise but a confident expression of faith based upon experience. He was assured of the continuing faithfulness of his heavenly Father. David was reminiscing and remembering times of great danger when he wrote, "I had fainted, unless I had believed to see the goodness of the Lᴏʀᴅ in the land of the living" (Ps. 27:13). He had always attended to the needs of his family and when persecution increased made arrangements for them to stay with the king of Moab (see 1 Sam. 22:3–4). It was probably during those difficult days that his parents became critical because his actions increased their problems. Then David discovered the abiding presence of God was of incalculable worth. God promised never to leave him, and David reciprocated by expressing a desire to live in the house of the Lord forever.

Many Gentile believers cannot appreciate the warmth and wonder of this text, but every Hebrew Christian knows its deep meaning. When an orthodox Jew accepts Christ as his Savior, the family sometimes holds a funeral service signifying a child has died.

God saw the unbelief which was spreading among Isaiah's despondent brethren and said, "But Zion said, The LORD hath forsaken me, and my Lord hath forgotten me. Can a woman forget her sucking child, that she should not have compassion on the son of her womb? yea, they may forget, yet will I not forget thee" (Isa. 49:14,15). That amazing statement suggests three facts.

God Cannot Cease Remembering Us

No mother could abandon her child unless unusual circumstances compelled her to do so. Unfortunately, newborn children are sometimes abandoned in a street or near an institution. God used this illustration to indicate He could never leave His children. At all times and in all places, God remembers the people who trust Him.

God Cannot Cease Loving Us

This is even more amazing. There is nothing unlovely about an innocent baby, but there is much that is detestable about men and women. That God loves people who oppose His will and resist His advances is almost unbelievable. That God could love even the people who crucified His Son defies understanding. The Lord said to Jeremiah, "I have loved thee with an everlasting love" (Jer. 31:3). It is difficult to comprehend the magnitude of this statement, but it indicates nothing can destroy divine love.

God Cannot Cease Helping Us

When David wrote, "When my father and my mother forsake me, then the LORD will take me up," he used an interesting word. Literally, the sentence says, "Then the LORD will gather me." The Savior expressed the same truth when, looking at Jerusalem, He said, ". . . how often would I have gathered thy children together, even as a hen gathereth her chickens under her wings, and ye would not" (Matt. 23:37).

> God feedeth the sparrows that fly in the air;
> they are never in trouble, but what He is there.
> If God with these creatures His blessings doth share,
> *then we surely can trust such infinite care.*

47

WHEN YOU HAVE HAD A GREAT EXPERIENCE, EXPECT PROBLEMS, BUT REMEMBER
2 CORINTHIANS 12:9

"And he said unto me, My grace is sufficient for thee."

Paul had many sensational experiences, but he was reluctant to speak of the greatest. He wrote, "I knew a man in Christ above fourteen years ago, (whether in the body, I cannot tell; or whether out of the body, I cannot tell: God knoweth;) . . . How that he was caught up into paradise, and heard unspeakable words which it is not lawful for a man to utter" (2 Cor. 12:2–4).

Even when he gave his testimony, Paul was more or less in a state of shock. Christians would like to know the details of that remarkable event. Did Paul see the Savior? Did he walk the streets of heaven and converse with glorified saints? Evidently he was instructed not to divulge what had been seen and heard.

Afterward he realized that if he became conceited, his mission to the Gentiles might be in jeopardy. He wrote, "And lest I should be exalted above measure through the abundance of the revelations, there was given to me a thorn in the flesh, the messenger of Satan to buffet me, lest I should be exalted above measure" (2 Cor. 12:7). Success is often the harbinger of problems, but humility is the mother of hope.

God's Favor . . . *A Definite Problem*

Only strong persons can overcome the danger created by success. Even blind people recognize an inflated ego, a detestable conceit, and the feeling of "being holier than thou." The Lord was wise when He placed a small child among His over-confident disciples and urged them to become childlike. Christian leaders should be aware of the dangers created by pride. When a member of a church lapses into sin, people may criticize. When a minister is guilty of horrendous sin, the damage done may never be repaired.

God's Forethought. . . *A Desperate Prayer*

Throughout the history of the church, scholars have speculated concerning the nature of Paul's "thorn in the flesh." Some of the earliest church leaders thought it to be a severe earache, or deafness, but the consensus is that Paul suffered from very poor eyesight which caused continuing problems. His difficulties became so severe that he had no time to boast about the revelations given in paradise. When his problems continued, he desperately prayed for help, and when answers were not forthcoming, he repeated his request. The Lord always answers prayer, but sometimes says, "No." When the apostle sought an explanation, God replied, "My grace is sufficient for thee." Christians should always remember God is too wise to make mistakes and too loving to be unkind.

God's Faithfulness . . . *A Delightful Promise*

> "The other evening I was riding home after a heavy day's work. I felt very weary and sore depressed, when swiftly and suddenly that text came to me: 'My grace is sufficient for thee.' I reached home and looked it up in the original, and at last it came to me in this way, 'My grace is sufficient for thee.' And I said, 'I should think it is, Lord,' and burst out laughing. I never fully understood what the holy laughter of Abraham was until then. It seemed to make unbelief so absurd. It was as though some little fish, being so thirsty, was troubled about drinking the river dry, and Father Thames said: 'Drink away, little fish, my stream is sufficient for thee.' Or it seemed that after seven years of plenty, a mouse feared it might die of famine, and Joseph might say, 'Cheer up, little mouse, my granaries are sufficient for thee.' Little faith will bring your souls to heaven; but great faith will bring heaven to your souls." —*Charles Haddon Spurgeon*

Writing to the Corinthians Paul said, "There hath no temptation taken you but such as is common to man: but God is faithful, who will not suffer you to be tempted above that ye are able; but will with the temptation also make a way to escape, that ye may be able to bear it" (1 Cor. 10:13). When Paul's burdens seemed to be heavy, he leaned more upon the everlasting arms of God's unfailing kindness. Annie Johnson Flint wrote:

> His grace is great enough to meet the great things:
> The crashing waves that overwhelm the soul,
> The roaring winds that leave us stunned and breathless,
> The sudden storms beyond our life's control.
> His grace is great enough to meet the small things:
> The little pin-prick troubles that annoy,
> The insect worries, buzzing and persistent,
> The squeaking wheels that grate upon our joy.

WHEN GOD SAYS NO, REMEMBER HE
MUST HAVE A REASON. ACTS 16:6–7

*Now when they had gone throughout Phrygia and the region
of Galatia, and were forbidden of the Holy Ghost to preach
the word in Asia, after they were come to Mysia, they assayed
to go into Bithynia but the Spirit suffered them not.*

One of the most disconcerting things in the world is the idea that God is either deaf or unconcerned with His people. To pray sincerely and apparently not be heard, to serve the Lord and be confronted by an impassable barrier, or to give of one's best and receive no cooperation from heaven is devastating. Inevitably the question arises, "Why has God done this to me?" Unless a person carefully and patiently waits for an answer, his or her soul may become embittered. Families often pray for the healing of a loved one, only to lose that person in death. A wife may pray for the salvation of her husband but face increasing intolerance. When God says no, He has a reason for so doing.

The Mystery of Closed Doors

Paul, the intrepid missionary, had problems! Seemingly, his efforts were fruitless; he had run into a wall! His party had traveled many miles and in spite of many difficulties had reached the populous areas of Asia. Pagans needed to hear the Gospel, but for some inscrutable reason, God had forbidden His servants to preach. Paul was frustrated. Why had the Lord brought him so far only to prevent him from telling the crowds about the Savior?

"They were forbidden of the Holy Ghost to preach the word in Asia." To be forbidden to preach in a village was disappointing, but at least another village could be found within a few miles. To be prevented from preaching the gospel in Asia meant a forced march of more than six hundred miles over difficult terrain before Paul could make his exit from the forbidden area.

"And a vision appeared to Paul in the night; There stood a man of Macedonia, and prayed him, saying, Come over into Macedonia, and help us. And after he had seen the vision, immediately we endeavoured to go into Macedonia" (Acts 16:9–10). When God closes a door in one place, He is often about to open a larger one elsewhere. When Elijah's brook dried up it became evident the Lord desired his presence in Zarephath (see 1 Kings 17:7–9).

The Misery of Continuing Doubt

Mary and Martha were very proud; Jesus of Nazareth had made their home a stopping place on the way to and from Jerusalem. His favorite food and Martha's expertise transformed every meal into a banquet. Then came tragedy and disillusionment. Lazarus became desperately ill, and his life was in jeopardy. "Therefore his sisters sent unto him, saying, Lord, behold he whom thou lovest is sick. When Jesus heard that, he said, This sickness is not unto death, but for the glory of God, that the Son of man might be glorified thereby. . . . When he had heard therefore that he was sick, he abode two days still in the same place where he was" (John 11:3–6).

It was incredible! Jesus had disregarded their appeal for help. Their Friend had refused to respond to their appeal. His preaching was more important than their pain! Could He not have come to their aid? Nothing would have been lost; the people would have followed Him, and His speech could have been concluded in Bethany. It was significant that even when He did come a few days later Mary still sat in the house. Delayed blessings sometimes transform despair into delight.

The Meaning of Certain Directions

The Wise Men were elated! Their long arduous journey was fulfilled with indescribable joy! They had seen the King! The scholars, who had been sufficiently wise to understand the message in the sky, had been even more wise to worship in a stable. Now, as had been previously arranged, they were ready to return to King Herod. The camels were rested, and the luggage was packed. Then, suddenly and unexpectedly, God said, "No." Those travelers were wise not to argue with the Lord. It became evident the new directions possibly: (a) preserved their lives because Herod might have ordered their execution; (b) prolonged their happiness because they did not participate in any plot to kill the infant Christ; (c) protected the Child who would be the salvation of a lost world.

They were in alignment with the will of the Almighty. When God said, "No," the lions were stilled as Daniel entered their den. The waves could not fall on the Hebrews who were fleeing from Pharaoh. It is wise to remember God always knows what He is doing. It is better to praise Him than to pout!

WHEN YOU ARE TEMPTED TO COMPROMISE, REMEMBER PROVERBS 3:5–6

*"Trust in the LORD with all thine heart; and lean not
unto thine own understanding. In all thy ways
acknowledge him, and he shall direct thy paths."*

It has often been said if a man does not stand for something, he will fall for anything! Some people are like reeds shaken by the wind. They yield to pressure from any direction! Perhaps that explains why corruption can be found in all walks of life. An official whose integrity remains unchallenged is a rare soul. The Bible describes Balaam as a prophet who compromised when a king offered to make him a wealthy man. From then on his increasing love for riches ruined his judgment, and even his donkey was wiser than he. Other important men exhibited similar tendencies and forfeited their claim to greatness.

The Wise Man . . . Solomon . . . *Who Became Sinful* (1 Kings 11:4–5)

Few people inherit fame and fortune, but of those who did Solomon was probably the most famous in the ancient world. He was born a prince and reared in luxury. Yet his excessive wealth seemed insignificant when compared with his wisdom. His phenomenal judgments and success in all matters of jurisprudence became known internationally. It was no great surprise when the Queen of Sheba came to verify the truthfulness of the reports circulating in her country.

She said, "It was a true report that I heard in mine own land of thy acts and of thy wisdom. Howbeit I believed not the words, until I came, and mine eyes had seen it: and, behold, the half was not told me: thy wisdom and prosperity exceedeth the fame which I heard" (1 Kings 10:6–7). It will forever remain a tragedy that the king who reached unprecedented heights of magnificence should be seduced and relegated to a realm of inexcusable shame. It was written of him, "For it came to pass, when Solomon was old, that his wives turned away his heart after other gods: and his heart was not perfect with the LORD his God, as was the heart of David his father. For Solomon went after Ashtoreth the goddess of the Zidonians, and after Milcom the abomination of the Ammonites" (1 Kings 11:4–5). Solomon leaned completely upon his own understanding, and his compromise ruined his integrity.

The Wealthy Man . . . The Ruler . . . *Who Became Sad* (Matthew 19:22)

He was the most admired citizen in town. Young, considerate, and exceptionally wealthy, he owned a great estate and was generous to his employees. He was deeply religious and lived according to the highest standards of morality. Guileless, sincere, and yet aristocratic, he was a man of exceptional credibility. "Good Master, what good thing shall I do, that I may have eternal life?" (Matt. 19:16).

The listeners who heard the Savior's reply probably frowned. "If thou wilt be perfect, go and sell that thou hast, and give to the poor, and thou shalt have treasure in heaven: and come and follow me" (Matt. 19:21). The young man was stunned! Momentarily, he saw strangers living in his beautiful home and heard new voices issuing orders while he, staff in hand, walked along dusty roads wondering how and where his next meal would be coming from. Revulsion shook his body. The Teacher was forcing a choice. What should he do?

"But when the young man heard that saying, he went away sorrowful: for he had great possessions" (Matt. 19:22). Poor man! He compromised. Although he desired to walk with Christ, he turned and went the other way. He did not realize Jesus was testing him, even as God tested Abraham when He asked that Isaac be sacrificed on Mount Moriah (see Gen. 22). Unfortunately the rich young ruler remained a wealthy pauper. Anything that takes precedence over Christ is too expensive no matter what it's worth!

The Weakening Man . . . Demas . . . *Who Became Side-Tracked* (2 Timothy 4:10)

Christians would like to know more about Demas who was mentioned three times in the epistles of Paul. Philemon 24 reveals he was a fellow-worker with Paul, Mark, Luke and Aristarchus. The letter to the Colossians informs that he was still with Paul and Luke, but nothing more was said of him. There was no commendation either of the man or his work.

The message to Timothy tells how he became a victim of worldly pleasure and deserted his companion. These phases in the life of Demas might be summarized as serving, sighing, and slipping! He became disillusioned as day after day he ministered to a prisoner in chains. Rome had many attractions; the gaiety of the city contrasted strangely with the gloom of the cell. The lust of his eyes and the yearning of his soul increased until finally he abandoned his friend.

Deep sorrow filled the soul of the apostle when he wrote, "Demas hath forsaken me, having loved this present world" (2 Tim. 4:10). Demas sought for pleasure, but lost his peace. It would be interesting to know his thoughts when his turn came to meet the Savior.

CONDITIONAL PROMISES

"And he said, Oh let not the Lord be angry, and I will speak yet
but this once: Peradventure ten shall be found there. And God said,
I will not destroy it for ten's sake. And the LORD went his way,
as soon as he had left communing with Abraham" (Gen. 18:32–33).

Sodom was a city infamous for its homosexuality. It seems inexplicable that Lot should be content to reside there. The apostle Peter described him as "just Lot, vexed with the filthy conversation of the wicked: (For that righteous man dwelling among them, in seeing and hearing, vexed his righteous soul from day to day with their unlawful deeds)" (2 Peter 2:7–8). It must be admitted that although he was displeased with the conduct of the Sodomites, Lot lacked the motivation to move away from the city. Why he permitted his two daughters to marry homosexuals remains a mystery. They became slaves, preparing meals, not women producing children. That such a city could exist after the flood indicates the extent to which people still ignored the laws of God.

The "If" of God's Mercy

Ahraham was the man who stood between Sodom and its complete destruction. The inhabitants were unworthy of anyone who interceded for their preservation. Even God had no delight in their fate. The conversation the Lord had with Abraham revealed that even He desired to find a way by which to spare the sinful people of Sodom. Their lewd and regrettable conduct was an affront to His righteousness, and their filthy conversation was a source of irritation to Lot.

Why did Lot continue to stay among such people when it was possible to walk away? It probably would have meant economic disaster. The fields of Sodom were fertile. He thought more of his wealth than of spiritual health. The filthy stories told by the men of Sodom were as thorns in his flesh—they "vexed his righteous soul" day and night! It became evident that God would sever a limb in order to save a body! He would destroy Sodom to save humanity. Yet if there were a way to avoid retribution, God was anxious to find it.

The "If" of God's Man

Abraham was the friend of God, and, therefore it was not a cause for amazement when the Lord informed him of the impending destruction. The response of the patriarch indicates certain facts: (a) Sincere prayer is always heard by God. It is never a waste of time; (b) Sincere prayer is always tenacious. Abraham did not abandon his efforts. When apparently his efforts failed, he tried again; (c) Sincere prayer always ascertains God's decisions are correct. Abraham began by mentioning the possibility of finding fifty righteous men within the city; his last plea spoke only of ten. Evidently it was impossible to find any! God knew this from the beginning; Abraham did not.

The destruction of Sodom was an act of mercy toward the entire human race. God removed a cancer which threatened the survival of man. The repeated use of the word "if" revealed the tenacity of the intercessor who tried to save Sodom and the wonderful mercy of God who listened to repeated requests.

The "If" of God's Message

Beginning with the possibility of finding fifty righteous men within the city, Abraham finally reduced the number to just ten. When it became evident that God knew what He was doing, the patriarch ceased to intercede. The city was entirely committed to evil. Civic pride and concern for morality did not exist. Every man did what was right in his own eyes. When work ended for the day, people sat in the gate discussing the details of their lewd conduct—telling, and retelling sordid details of their homosexual acts and looking for any unfortunate visitor upon whom they could exercise their abominable desires.

Abraham's nephew sat listening to the filthy conversations, and he too might have perished had not his uncle prayed for his safety. "And it came to pass, when God destroyed the cities of the plain, that God remembered Abraham, and sent Lot out of the midst of the overthrow, when he overthrew the cities in the which Lot dwelt" (Gen. 19:29). The use of the word "if" reveals there is a limit even to the mercy of God. Although He made promises to Abraham, the Lord was denied the opportunity to fulfill any one of them. People who exclude God from their daily routine can only blame themselves when their possessions go up in flames!

57

*"And Moses made a serpent of brass, and put it upon a pole,
and it came to pass, that if a serpent had bitten any man,
when he beheld the serpent of brass, he lived" (Num. 21:9).*

We may never know how often Jesus of Nazareth studied the Scriptures. As a developing child, He had the capacity to learn, yet as the Son of God He knew everything. As a boy, He diligently unwrapped the scrolls to read, As the One sent from God, He knew the content of every scroll. He had given their message to the prophets. If Jesus had a favorite story, it might have been the one which described the serpent in the wilderness. That He should use it to instruct Nicodemus was exceptionally thought provoking.

A Terrible Catastrophe

As far as the eye could see, the scene was heartrending—thousands of people lay dead or dying on the ground as innumerable serpents slithered over their prostrate bodies. The sounds of moaning filled the air, and pitiable cries for help affected even the most hard-hearted people. The Israelites had become victims of arrogance, and their ceaseless complaints were an offense to God. Then "the people came to Moses, and said, We have sinned, for we have spoken against the LORD, and against thee; pray unto the LORD that he may take away the serpents from us. And Moses prayed for the people" (21:7).

It was a cause for regret that the tribes substituted criticism for gratitude. They forgot to praise the Lord for blessings and used their time to express the displeasure of their embittered souls. It was tragic that many people postponed their request for forgiveness until it was too late even to pray.

A Thrilling Capability

"And the Lord said unto Moses, Make thee a fiery serpent and set it upon a pole: and it shall come to pass, that every one that is bitten, when he looketh upon it, shall live" (21:8). Whether or not the stricken Hebrews knew the significance of the brazen serpent is questionable; their survival did not depend upon theological understanding but upon simple faith. When they were told to look and live, they did not debate whether or not it would be wise or foolish to obey the instructions. Fiery serpents had endangered their lives, but the serpent on the pole was dead. Symbolically, the power of the serpents had been destroyed; the venom had become harmless. The miracle had been accomplished without human aid. The Hebrews' only part in the miraculous process was a sincere request for assistance. God had provided an unparalleled way of escape, but there was need for haste—the dangerous venom was already within their veins.

A Tremendous Choice

When someone shouted, "Look and live!", wise people did as they were told. If stubborn people refused to open their eyes or looked in another direction, they exhibited stupidity and deserved to die. God's command given through Moses was explicit. He had provided a miraculous way of deliverance, but healing was conditional. If people looked, they lived; if they did not, they perished. Choice was mandatory, and their salvation depended on what they decided to do.

Is it too much to imagine delivered people running around the crowd, lifting sick people in their arms, or helping them to sit up as the cry echoed around the camp—"Look and live!"? Perhaps New Testament evangelists would have described that ancient scene as the first evangelistic service. Yet even then God did not act without the cooperation of men and women.

A Triumphant Conclusion

The Lord saw again what happened centuries earlier, and was thrilled when He remembered how grateful people said to stricken neighbors, "He did it for me; He can do it for you! Look and live!" When the disciples went forth to evangelize the world, they probably used that remarkable story mentioned by their Master. They urged listeners to look to the Cross where in the Person of their Lord the old serpent, the Devil, had been defeated. It is wise to remember that in a changing world the Gospel of God's grace remains unchangeable.

"Behold, when we come into the land, thou shalt bind this line of scarlet thread in the window which thou didst let us down by: and thou shalt bring thy father, and thy mother, and thy brethren, and all thy father's household, home unto thee. And if thou utter this our business, then we will be quit of thine oath which thou hast made us to swear" (Josh. 2:18, 20).

This is one of the most intriguing stories in the Bible. Pastor Robert Daugherty says, "It tells of a woman who went from 'Sin's House of Shame to the Savior's Hall of Fame.'" Rahab was one of the most notorious people in Jericho. She lived in a house built upon or into the surrounding wall of the city, and since she was a professional prostitute, citizens disregarded the two strange men who one day entered her place of business. Yet, God was interested in that strange woman. Perhaps the citizens of Jericho were too preoccupied with thoughts of the advancing Israelites to consider from where the strangers came. How this woman hid and protected the Hebrew spies makes exciting reading. The reward given to her revealed the fact that no individual is beyond the reach of God's grace, and no task too difficult for the power of the Lord to accomplish.

Her Obvious Fear

The news of the approaching Hebrews had paralyzed the citizens of Jericho. The impending fall of the city had filled them with dread. All businesses had closed, and the elders of the city were bewildered. Then, someone remembered the strangers and inquired about their whereabouts. Were they still with the woman who lived on the wall? When they asked Rahab for information, she lied to protect the visitors, and perhaps for the first time in her life she ceased to think about financial remuneration.

Her Outgoing Friendliness

How she protected the fugitives indicated a sudden change in her outlook. It would be better to be alive and poor than to be a wealthy corpse! Regardless of the outcome, she was determined to obey the instructions of the men whom she had sheltered. She had no moral nor religious claim for protection, but the men of Israel had spoken of a scarlet thread to be hung from her window.

Her kind deeds, though appreciated by her friends, could not guarantee safety. Her faith and obedience offered what nothing else could. She remembered how the man emphasized, "And *if* thou utter this our business, then we will be quit of thine oath which thou hast made us to swear." The fulfillment of the promise was conditional. Argument would have been foolish. God's servants had spoken; wisdom dictated obedience. She hung the thread in the window and then confidently waited.

Her Observant Faith

"And she said, According unto your words, so be it. And she sent them away, and they departed: and she bound the scarlet line in the window" (Josh. 2:21). Did the men see the scarlet thread in Rahab's house? Did they pull it from some fabric that she possessed or carefully extract it from their own garments?

That information was never revealed. Perhaps the woman was unable to understand the implications of the strange promise, but evidently she believed what had been told. Salvation depended upon her obedience and the veracity of God's promise. Every student of the Scriptures recognizes the connection between the deliverance of this woman and the redemption of the Hebrew slaves in Egypt. They sheltered behind the scarlet stain on the doors of their homes, Rahab behind the thread in her window. Throughout the Scripture scarlet is indicative of sacrifice. These incidents show that salvation is only through the sacrifice of Christ. Blessed is the person who believes, obeys, and rests upon the promises of God.

Her Outstanding Fellowship

It is now believed that Jericho was destroyed by an earthquake; the walls fell outward. Rahab's house was either on or in the wall and would ordinarily have been destroyed. Evidently God knew how to protect those who believed His promises. Rahab's subsequent marriage to Salmon, one of the spies she protected, and the birth of their child revealed the magnitude of God's grace. How she became a link in the royal lineage which led to the Messiah is one of the most atonishing stories in the Bible (see Matt. 1:5).

JEPHTHAH, WHO MADE AND KEPT
A PROMISE HE REGRETTED

*"And Jephthah vowed a vow unto the LORD, and said, If thou shalt
without fail deliver the children of Ammon into mine hands, Then it shall
be, that whatsoever cometh forth of the doors of mine house to meet me,
when I return in peace from the children of Ammon, shall surely be the
LORD's, and I will offer it up for a burnt offering" (Judg. 11:30–31).*

Jephthah was the son of an prostitute (see Judg. 11:1) who was
later expelled by his half-brothers because they considered his presence a reproach to the family. Yet the neighbors never forgot the
tremendous strength of the fugitive who became the leader of a
band of outlaws in the land of Tob (see Judg. 11:3). When enemies
threatened to devastate the Gileadites and the people urgently requested the aid of the outcast, Jephthah regained all he had previously lost. At the head of his army he prepared to confront the
enemy, but the influence of the people among whom he had lived
made him do something that he regretted for the rest of his life. He
promised to give to God the first thing that came from his house to
congratulate him on his victory. The sacrifice of human beings was
not permitted in Israel, but unfortunately Jephthah had lived too
long among pagans.

The Irresponsible Promise

Vows were sacred in Israel; people were not encouraged to make
them unless they had every intention to fulfill their obligation. Evidently Jephthah was uncertain of the outcome of the forthcoming
battle, and his irrational vow resembled a bribe. He was saying, "O
God, if you will grant victory to me in this battle, I will give a
wonderful gift to you." He never paused to consider that God neither
desired nor requested such a promise. The battle was the Lord's;
Jephthah was only the commander-in-chief of operations. He was
very sincere but had neither the right nor authority to jeopardize the
life of his only child. Abraham Lincoln once said, "It is better to
remain silent and be thought a fool, than to speak and remove all
doubt."

The Irrepressible Pain

The enemy had been vanquished; the victor was returning to
receive the cheers of his people. It was customary for a conqueror

to be met by a band of female singers (see 1 Sam. 18:6–7), but evidently on this occasion the lovely daughter of the victorious Jephthah was either a member or the leader of the celebrating minstrels (Judg. 11:34). She was the first to emerge from the home of Jephthah, and her appearance troubled her father.

"And it came to pass, when he saw her, that he rent his clothes, and said, Alas, my daughter! thou hast brought me very low, and thou art one of them that trouble me: for I have opened my mouth unto the LORD, and I cannot go back. And she said unto him, My father, if thou hast opened thy mouth unto the LORD, do to me according to that which hath proceeded out of thy mouth" (Judg. 11:35–36). She became a victim of her father's folly.

The Irremovable Problem

The girl's fate has occasioned debate throughout the ages. Shocked by the idea of a merciless human sacrifice, theologians have tried to explain the vow as a commitment to a religious order associated with the tabernacle rather than a blood sacrifice. Since she became a celibate, they bewailed her virginity; she would never become a mother.

This interpretation may be very attractive, but entering an order could hardly be desribed as a burnt offering! Unger wrote, "The victim was led to the altar by the person offering it, duly consecrated by the laying on of hands, and then slain by the offerer. The priest then took the blood, and sprinkled it round about upon the altar" *(Unger's Bible Dictionary*, p. 948, Moody Press).

The Irreproachable Procession

When Jephthah slew his daughter, anguish spread through the tribes; people recognized the folly of that unhappy parent, and knew he had become a victim of his own impetuosity. The brave young woman who preferred death to dishonor became a heroine in Israel, and every year her female admirers convened ceremonies which lasted four days. They perpetuated the memory of one of their number whose selflessness made her immortal. To break any vow made to God is to be unreliable and a liar. Jephthah's experience should restrain all people whose enthusiasm makes their tongues too active.

> *"And [Hannah] vowed a vow, and said, O Lᴏʀᴅ of hosts, if thou wilt indeed look on the affliction of thine handmaid, and remember me, and not forget thine handmaid, but wilt give unto thine handmaid a man child, then I will give him unto the Lᴏʀᴅ all days of his life, and there shall no razor come upon his head" (1 Sam. 1:11).*

A nagging woman can be a pest! Her tongue is as sharp as a razor, her taunting glances as infuriating as anything upon earth, and her presence a deep-seated thorn in the flesh! This was all apparent in the home of a man named Elkanah who had two wives. Unfortunately Peninnah, the mother of his children, had not captured his heart.

"And he had two wives; the name of the one was Hannah, and the name of the other Peninnah: and Peninnah had children, but Hannah had no children" (1 Sam. 1:2). The mother was very observant. When she saw affection for her rival shining in the eyes of her husband, jealousy filled her soul. Her scathing words erupted as lava from a volcanic soul. "And her adversary (Peninnah) also provoked her sore, for to make her fret, because the Lᴏʀᴅ had shut up her womb. And as . . . she went up to the house of the Lᴏʀᴅ, so she provoked her; therefore she (Hannah) wept, and did not eat" (1:Sam. 1:6–7).

The Unrevealed Plan . . . *The Strange Delay*

There are times when the silence of God is incomprehensible. When He answers prayer affirmatively, believers respond with overwhelming joy. When the reply is negative, sadness and disappointment become evident. But when prayers are apparently ignored–that can be devastating.

In such circumstances Hannah first appears in biblical history. She was a victim of the common belief that childlessness was a curse from God, that barren wombs were a reproach, that God had pronounced such women as being unworthy to become mothers. Hannah's sorrow was intensified when the other woman in the home seized every opportunity to humiliate her. She hugged her children, made them attractive garments, and used them as arrows to pierce Hannah's soul. The desperate lady sought God's help, but He appeared to be indifferent to her problems. She did not know she was playing the chief role in one of the greatest dramas ever witnessed by angels. God knew He would respond to her prayers, but delayed His response. An unanswered prayer is not an indication He is deaf. God loves to surprise His people!

The Unexpected Promise . . . *The Surprising Decision*

Eli, the priest at Shiloh, was an elderly man who assumed too much! "As she continued praying before the LORD, that Eli marked her mouth. Now Hannah, she spake in her heart; only her lips moved, but her voice was not heard: therefore Eli thought she had been drunken" (1 Sam. 1:12–13).

Hannah had a broken heart and a burdened soul. Although God remained silent, she refused to cease praying. She could have become angry with the unsympathetic priest; but he was the anointed of God, and his mistake could not justify her anger. "And she vowed a vow, and said, O LORD of hosts *if* thou wilt indeed look on the affliction of thine handmaid, and remember me, and not forget thine handmaid, but wilt give unto thine handmaid and remember me, and not forget thine handmaid, but wilt give unto thine handmaid a man child, then I will give him unto the LORD all the days of his life" (1 Sam. 1:11).

When that faithful woman made her vow, excitement probably spread through heaven, and God whispered, "At last." She desired a son to quiet her adversary. God desired a Savior to quicken His people. She had been waiting for the Lord. He had been waiting for her! His continuing silence had been another expression of great wisdom. As the poet wrote, "God moves in a mysterious way, His wonders to perform."

The Unbroken Promise . . . *The Sublime Deliverer*

"And the Lord remembered her . . . and when she had weaned him . . . and brought the child to Eli . . . she said, O my lord, I am the woman that stood by thee here, praying unto the LORD. For this child I prayed; and the LORD hath given me my petition which I asked of him. Therefore I have lent him unto the LORD; as long as he liveth he shall be lent to the LORD, and he worshipped the LORD there" (1 Sam. 1:19–28).

It has always been impossible to outgive God. Hannah fulfilled her vow and was rewarded in ways she thought to be impossible (see 1 Sam. 2:21). No doubt she received news of her son, for whenever a traveler arrived she heard of the phenomenal child to whom God was revealing Himself in Shiloh. "But Samuel ministered before the LORD, being a child, girded with a linen ephod" (1 Sam. 2:18).

The subsequent history of that dedicated boy is now known to all readers of the Bible. His inspiring influence, sane counsel, and dedicated leadership saved a nation from degradation and decay. He became God's man in difficult times.

"And it came to pass, when they were gone over, that Elijah said unto Elisha, Ask what I shall do for thee, before I be taken away from thee. And Elisha said, I pray thee, let a double portion of thy spirit be upon me. And he said, Thou hast asked a hard thing, nevertheless, if thou see me when I am taken from thee, it shall be so unto thee; but if not, it shall not be so" (2 Kings 2:9–10).

Elisha would never forget the day when the prophet Elijah passed the field in which he was plowing. His call to succeed the illustrious prophet was as sudden as it was remarkable. The local people remembered the sumptuous banquet they enjoyed when Elisha "took a yoke of oxen, and slew them, and boiled their flesh with the instruments of the oxen, and gave unto the people, and they did eat. Then he (Elisha) arose, and went after Elijah, and ministered unto him" (1 Kings 19:21). But the time for parting had arrived. The master's face shone with a new expectancy. He was going home!

The Suggestive Request

Elisha refused to be "a drop-out!" There were schools for the young prophets at Bethel and Gilgal. In either place Elisha could have found food and fellowship. That he refused to accept the invitation given to him indicated such things were unattractive. He "had set his heart on things above, and not on the things of earth." The scene described by the historian suggested how the Messiah would someday go through the waters of death and ascend into heaven. The falling mantle represented the descent of the Holy Spirit, and Elisha's return to the Jordan River indicated that, although the church was crucified with Christ, it needed to return to its waters. This indicates how the truth of identification with Christ in death would become experiential—Christians would need to die daily! Such blessing would only become real when the disciples refused to become drop-outs!

The Stubborn Response

The repeated requests made by the sons of the prophets revealed the intensity of their desire. They wanted fellowship with a man who had been Elijah's companion. He could teach them, and they could help him. Elisha's refusal negated all their desires. The subsequent story revealed Elisha's preeminent wish. As Solomon, in similar circumstances desired wisdom, Elisha requested a double portion of Elijah's spirit. To obtain that incalculable treasure, he would have followed the prophet to the end of the earth.

The Special Reward

There were many sons of the prophets, and evidently they were informed and sincere. Yet, to Elisha alone was the mantle of Elijah given; apparently, no other man wanted it! The prophet's answer to his servant's request contained the conditional word "if."

"Thou hast asked a hard thing; nevertheless *if* thou see me when I am taken from thee, it shall be so unto thee; but if not, it shall not be so" (2 Kings 2:10). It is thought provoking to modern readers that Elisha received exactly what he desired. He requested a double portion of his master's spirit and, ultimately, performed twice as many miracles as were performed by Elijah. That was not a coincidence. What might have happened had he requested ten times the amount? His desire was probably influenced by the birthright given to the first born in every family. The eldest son inherited twice as much as any other child. However, it was not the size of the bequest which mattered, but the intensity of Elisha's longing. He could have requested anything in existence, but the entire world was secondary to the power of God. What he was to Israel and what the early Christians meant to their world, we can be to our generation if the same intensity of purpose dominates our aspirations. Drop outs only succeed in getting nowhere!

The Sublime Recipient

"He took up also the mantle of Elijah that fell from him, and went back, and stood by the bank of Jordan . . . and when he had smitten the waters, they parted hither and thither: and Elisha went over" (2 Kings 2:13–14). No other prophet of God was so Christlike. Elisha raised the dead (2 Kings 4:35–37), cleansed a leper (2 Kings 5:14), gave sight to the blind (2 Kings 6:20), fed the hungry (2 Kings 4:42–44), and life was given through his death (2 Kings 13:21). Many "sons of the prophets" believe in the fullness of God's power but are not prepared to go all the way to get it!

"If my people, which are called by my name, shall humble themselves, and pray, and seek my face, and turn from their wicked ways; then will I hear from heaven, and will forgive their sins, and will heal their land" (2 Chron. 7:14).

Solomon was elated and yet humbled. The magnificent temple had been completed. The eyes of the workmen shone with justifiable pride, and the roof, glistening in the sunshine, seemed to suggest the glory of the living God was upon Israel. Perhaps even the angels were filled with holy admiration. "And the LORD appeared to Solomon by night, and said unto him, I have heard thy prayer, and have chosen this place to myself for an house of sacrifice" (7:12). Then the Lord proceeded to make a covenant in which two vital words were used three times. "If" Israel would do certain things, "then" the Lord would do more for them than could be imagined.

A Sincere Penitence . . . *"Shall Humble Themselves"*

This verse has been one of the most quoted of all Bible texts. It has been a ray of brilliance shining over the troubled waters of church history. The Savior said He would build His church and promised the gates of hell would not prevail against it (see Matt. 16:18). Nevertheless, there have been occasions when the church was powerless, when its existence seemed to be in jeopardy. Then God sent revival among His people, and the fire of a new enthusiasm became evident. The desire for such visitations never diminished, and all people who seek a spiritual renewal remember the promise made to Solomon. God outlined the necessary requirements for such divine visitations, and the first was the need for penitence in the hearts of His people. People who are too proud to kneel are too weak to stand!

A Simple Prayer . . . *"And Pray"*

Prayer is the breath of a believer; pride is the paralysis of a dying soul. The Pharisee prayed and succeeded in getting nowhere; the publican prayed from the back seat in the synagogue and reached the heart of God (see Luke 18:10–14). When a church or an individual kneels before the Almighty, God is reminded of human frailty, desire, and trust. When Evan Roberts, the Welsh revivalist, knelt in a field and prayed throughout the night, he was transformed, and later with God's help he changed his country. A person who never prays advertises his or her self-sufficiency. A church without a prayer meeting is a mausoleum with many occupants! Revivals cannot be worked up, but they can be prayed down! Solomon's temple was accepted as a place of sacrifice and worship. It was never used for bingo, money-raising events, and secular gatherings. Within the sanctuary people prayed; outside, they put into practice what they had learned inside!

A Special Project . . . *"And Seek My Face"*

To seek anything indicates an intense desire, a determination to persevere until what is being sought is found. The person who abandons his or her search prematurely indicates a decreasing intensity of desire—"but if from thence thou shalt seek the Lord thy God, thou shalt find him, if thou seek him with all thy heart and with all thine soul." (Deut. 4:29). It is thought-provoking that of the five hundred people who saw the risen Christ only one hundred twenty remained until the Day of Pentecost (see 1 Cor. 15:6 and Acts 1:15). Clouds of doubt may fill the sky, but in seeking the face of God people should persevere until night has ended and the Sun of Righteousness has arisen "with healing in his wings" (Mal. 4:2).

A Serious Purpose . . . *"And Turn from Their Wicked Ways"*

This has always been the most important prerequisite for revival. A dairy would never place milk into cartons or bottles filled with cobwebs. Neither will God place His Holy Spirit into hearts filled with secret sin. No man can worship an idol and, at the same time, adore the Savior. God promised that "if" Israel conformed to His will, "then" He would heal their land. Today's world is filled with hatred; the church is torn by moral laxity, and individuals who once thrilled the heart of God now grieve Him.

Many years ago the question was asked, "Can God furnish a table in the wilderness?" The reply was affirmative; he did so every day for forty years. A similar question could still be asked: "Can God revive the church in a decadent world?" The answer must be "yes," but the old condition still applies. "If" my people will . . . "then" will I heal their land! People pray for a revival, but forget it begins within individuals. A person may be unable to change the world or revolutionize his or her church, but if one is not interested in quickening oneself, his or her prayers are worthless.

O God, send a revival, and let it begin in me.

*"So the merchants and sellers of all kind of ware lodged without
Jerusalem once or twice. Then I testified against them, and
said unto them, Why lodge ye about the wall? if ye do so again,
I will lay hands on you. From that time forth came they no
more on the sabbath" (Neh. 13:20–21).*

Nehemiah was very angry and determined; his associates knew
he meant business! The Hebrews had returned from Babylon, and
inspired by their leader, had repaired the walls of Jerusalem and re-
commenced the temple services. For a time it seemed the nation
was about to enjoy a spiritual awakening, but circumstances neces-
sitated the return of Nehemiah to Babylon. He was probably expected to report on the progress being made in Palestine.

Unfortunately, during his absence all kinds of forbidden things
were allowed to thrive. The sabbath became a market day. Israel's
greatest enemy was given an apartment in the sanctuary, and inter-
marriage with heathens became popular. Returning from Babylon,
Nehemiah was horrified to see what had taken place during his
absence but determined to restore order. He assumed control of the
city, and the way he handled the task was remarkable. He expelled
the enemy from the temple, condemned the illicit marriages of the
people, and threatened sabbath breakers with violence. His fierce
assault scared the merchants, and they "came no more on the sabbath." The account of the efforts of that great reformer should teach
valuable lessons.

A Required Obedience

Prosperity can be dangerous to the people of God. They are often
more faithful in adversity. It was written, "But Jeshurun waxed fat,
and kicked: thou art waxen fat, thou art grown thick, thou art covered with fatness; then he forsook God which made him, and lightly
esteemed the Rock of his salvation" (Deut. 32:15). This has been
evident throughout the ages. When oppressed, men pray for help;
when prosperous, they forget from where their aid came. Nehemiah
was the conscience of the nation. When he was present, people
were reminded of their sacred obligations; when he was absent they
became unfaithful and forgot God's promises were conditional. The
Lord's benediction fell upon pathways of righteousness; if Israel

walked elsewhere, they walked in darkness and were beyond the reach of His blessings. Many centuries later John wrote, "But *if* we walk in the light, as he is in the light, we have fellowship one with another" (1 John 1:7). He also write, "*If* we . . . walk in darkness, we lie, and do not the truth" (1 John 1:6). People who expect God to fulfill His promises should never forsake His paths.

A Resolute Obsession

A missionary from Central Africa told the following story. Electricity had been introduced to the mission station and, to honor the native pastor, arrangements had been made to install it in his hut. It was to be a great occasion, and tribesmen had gathered to celebrate the event. The pastor's wife had cleaned her house, and the moment to press the switch had arrived. When the light began to shine, the oohs and aahs of the people were understandable, but suddenly the pastor's wife rushed out of her hut shouting, "Don't come in here, don't come in here. I thought my house was clean until that light came on!" Nehemiah's cleansing of his city was thorough and complete. Had he been half-hearted in his endeavor, the blessing of God would have been denied. To keep the temple clean should be a priority with every worshiper. John probably had this thought in mind when he wrote, "walk in the light as He is in the light." It is wonderful to believe in Christ but better to be like Him.

A Remarkable Outcome

Flavius Josephus wrote of Nehemiah's work, "When the nations which dwelt in Syria heard that the building of the wall was finished, they had indignation at it; but when Nehemiah saw that the city was thin of people, he exhorted the priests and the Levites that they would leave the country, and remove themselves to the city, and there continue. And he built them houses at his own expense. So when Nehemiah had done many other excellent things, and things worthy of commendation in a glorious manner, he came to a great age and then died. He was a man of good and righteous disposition, and very ambitious to make his own nation happy, and he hath left the walls of Jerusalem as an eternal monument for himself." (*Antiquities of the Jews*, Book 11, Chapter 5) Anything done for God is worth doing well!

*"Even the youths shall faint and be weary, and the young men
shall utterly fall: But they that wait upon the LORD shall renew their
strength; they shall mount up with wings as eagles; they shall run,
and not be weary; and they shall walk, and not faint" (Isa. 40:30–31).*

Isaiah lived in troubled times when the threat of war was a
constant menace. The Babylonian empire was extending toward the
west; the northern kingdom of Israel had been conquered and its
people taken into captivity. To prevent the overthrow of Jerusalem,
Hezekiah paid tribute to Sennacherib. To supply the required three
hundred talents of silver and thirty talents of gold, treasures had
been removed from the sanctuary (see 2 Kings 18:14–16). The
prophet lived through that dangerous era and proved God was able
to protect His people. He saw people who were motivated by fear,
whose profession of faith was spontaneous and shallow. They desired to please the Lord, but their initial enthusiasm disappeared.
Isaiah supplied a vivid description of people who sincerely waited
upon the Lord.

Flying . . . An Initial Enthusiasm . . . *How Typical*

The eagle was the most famous bird known in the ancient world,
and because it molted and grew new feathers in old age, people
believed this to be a renewal of its youth. The eagle's swift ascent
and majestic progress indicated it was sovereign of the sky. Evidently, the prophet had seen similar characteristics among his neighbors. During times of urgent need people prayed for assistance, and
their initial response was an enthusiasm which took them as high as
the heavens. Nothing was impossible. The German commentators
Keil and Delitzsch state, "The proper rendering of the text is 'they
cause their wings to rise, or lift their wings high, like the eagles'"
(*Biblical Commentary on the Old Testament*, Vol. 7. William B.
Eerdmans, Grand Rapids, MI). There was nothing wrong about an
overwhelming enthusiasm for God and His kingdom. It was one of
the most exhilarating experiences known to man and the Old Testament equivalent of "the first love" (see Rev. 2:4). When the disciples ended a preaching mission with ecstacy, the Savior directed
their thoughts to an even greater happiness. He said ". . . rejoice
because your names are written in heaven" (see Luke 10:17–20).

73

Running . . . An Indefatigable Endurance . . . *How Thrilling*

For birds who know how to take advantage of air currents, flying is a simple matter; for humans, running is more difficult. It requires persistent perseverance and suggests an athlete determined to win a prize. Writing to the Galatian church, Paul said, "Ye did run well; who did hinder you that ye should not obey the truth?" (Gal. 5:7). A wonderful beginning to a race is great, but unless the runner completes the course, the effort is without merit.

Isaiah saw many who did not continue what had been commenced. The secret of success seemed to be expressed in his condition, "they that wait upon the Lord." Devoted people are not content with hearing the Lord's voice occasionally; they sit at His feet! Spiritual athletes do not begin with a tremendous burst of speed and after a while pause to enjoy a picnic beside the track. David knew the need of waiting upon the Lord and in Psalm 27:14 said, "Wait on the LORD: be of good courage, and he shall strengthen thine heart; wait, I say, on the LORD." Although the word *if* was not mentioned at that time, its conditional truth was present in David's mind. If people do not wait upon the Lord, their spiritual resources will be depleted.

Walking . . . An Inspired Example . . . *How Tremendous*

This is the ultimate in Christian experience: when Enoch walked with God, the Lord took him home! To walk with the Lord means stopping when He stops and continuing when He moves. People often say of their children, "They must crawl before they can walk, and they must walk before they can run." That is not so with God's babies! They can fly before they can run and run before they can walk. This path leads to spiritual maturity. Writing to the church at Sardis, the Lord said, "Thou hast a few names even in Sardis which have not defiled their garments; and they shall walk with me in white: for they are worthy" (Rev. 3:4). It was regrettable that to this assembly with its magnificent reputation, the Lord said, "Thou hast a name that thou livest, and art dead" (Rev. 3:1). Yet, even in Sardis there were believers who had not defiled their garments. They would walk with Christ in eternity as they had walked with Him on earth. No one can walk with the Lord and at the same time be far from Him.

THE HEBREW CAPTIVES AND THEIR
"IF" OF DEFIANCE

"If it be so, our God whom we serve is able to deliver us from the burning fiery furnace, and he will deliver us out of thine hand, O king. But if not, be it known unto thee, O king, that we will not serve thy gods, nor worship the golden image which thou hast set up" (Dan. 3:17–18).

Most eastern monarchs were self-made deities who worshiped at their own shrine! They made the law, and few, if any, of their subjects, opposed royal edicts. Monarchs were autocrats who never tolerated interference. It was amazing when three insignificant Hebrews disdained regal authority and defied the king of Babylon. Nebuchadnezzar was a proud man easily swayed by insincere praise. He was determined that opposition would never exist within his domain.

When challenged by three Hebrew slaves, his face became livid, and his anger flowed into a torrent of passion. The foreign upstarts had refused to worship his idol, and he considered their action to be a personal insult. Nevertheless, he suggested the offenders should be given another chance; the lads were immature and irresponsible and might be persuaded to change their decision. When the captives refused to obey his command, the king became furious. Indifferent to his threats, the young men proclaimed their faith in the Lord, and said, "He will deliver us out of thine hand, O king." Such defiance had never been known in Babylon!

Their Deep Concern . . . *Discerning*

There was no promise in the story. It was a statement of faith emanating from convictions. Whatever transpired, the king of Babylon would no longer control them. The God of the Hebrews could and would deliver His servants from the huge fire—if He so desired. Yet, even if deliverance were decreed, He would ultimately liberate them from slavery in Babylon. They believed the unspoken promise of God, and their faith destroyed the fear of death. They knew life would lose its joy if they were troubled by a guilty conscience. It was preferable to die with honor than to live in shame. The Lord would not disappoint them in their hour of need; but if for unknown reasons He permitted them to be incinerated, they would endure their trial of faith courageously. It would be better to die for God than live without Him.

Their Definite Confession . . . *Declaring*

Our God whom we serve is able to deliver us, but if not, *we will not serve thy gods* (see Dan. 3:16–17). Unbelievers would have called them stubborn, and friends might have described them as foolish, but angels would have proclaimed them to be saints. Any suggestion that they recant was disdainfully rejected. Any other action would have diappointed God, displeased their brethren, and destroyed their happiness. Their decision was decisive, definite, and delightful. It infuriated the king of Babylon and thrilled the King of heaven. When they remained true to their convictions, they had no verbal promise of deliverance nor expectation of the Savior awaiting them in the middle of the furnace. They seemed to say, "Nebuchadnezzar, this is what we believe. This is what we shall do."

Their Delightful Companion . . . *Delivering*

"Then Nebuchadnezzar the king was astonished, and rose up in haste, and spake, and said unto his counsellors, Did not we cast three men bound into the midst of the fire? They answered and said unto the king, True, O king. He answered and said, Lo, I see four men loose, walking in the midst of the fire, and they have no hurt; and the form of the fourth is like the Son of God" (Dan. 3:24–25).

As photographs are developed in a dark room, so the clearest and best pictures of the Savior are produced in the darkest experiences of life. The Hebrew captives would have been utterly impoverished had they not been cast into that fire. The circumstances which threatened destruction brought immortality. The fire of Nebuchadnezzar introduced them experimentally and personally to the Prince of heaven. They would have appreciated the words spoken by Moses, "Out of heaven he made thee to hear his voice, that he might instruct thee: and upon earth he shewed thee his great fire; and thou heardest his words out of the midst of the fire" (Deut. 4:36). It is refreshing to remember that either in or out of the fiery problems of life, the grace and power of God are sufficient to meet the needs of all people who believe in the promises of the Almighty.

"Bring ye all the tithes into the storehouse, that there may be meat in mine house, and prove me now herewith, saith the LORD of hosts, if I will not open you the windows of heaven, and pour you out a blessing, that there shall not be room enough to receive it" (Mal. 3:10).

Malachi was the prophet whom God commissioned to help Nehemiah. He appeared at an opportune moment, for in all probability Ezra, Nehemiah's friend, had died. Much of what had been gained by the reformers was being lost. The return from Babylon had been triumphantly completed. The walls of Jerusalem had been rebuilt, and it seemed the Hebrews were about to regain some of their former grandeur. Then it became necessary for Nehemiah to return to Babylon. What he found when he returned to Jerusalem was heartbreaking. Eliashib, the priest, had become an ally of Tobiah, Israel's greatest enemy. Disregarding the commandments of God, an apartment had been given him within the temple. Nehemiah wrote, "And I came to Jerusalem, and understood of the evil that Eliashib did for Tobiah, in preparing him a chamber in the courts of the house of God. And it grieved me sore: therefore I cast forth all the household stuff of Tobiah out of the chamber" (Neh. 13:7–8).

The Abominable Decadence

When he returned, Nehemiah was horrified to see the deterioration among the children of Israel. The ministers in the temple had become indifferent. They offered polluted bread upon God's altar, presented imperfect sacrifices, and every person associated with the temple services could be bribed.

Apparently, no one rendered any service unless payment was received. Malachi said, "Who is there even among you, that would shut the doors for nought? neither do ye kindle fire on mine altar for nought. I have no pleasure in you, saith the LORD of hosts" (Mal. 1:10). Evidently, even the high priest had succumbed to the attractiveness of financial reward and had permitted a heathen to reside in the sanctuary.

The Awful Devastation

This conduct and the continuing indifference of Israel brought judgment upon their fields. Crops failed, fruit withered on the trees, and harvests failed. Farmers worked hard and reaped nothing. The blight of God's judgment rested upon the nation, and the future seemed ominous. It appeared as though the Lord had forsaken His people, but actually they had forsaken Him. It was at this point in history God sent a new prophet named Malachi who denounced the sins of the people but conveyed a new promise from God. He said, "Bring ye all the tithes into the storehouse, that there may be meat in mine house, and prove me now herewith saith the LORD of hosts, if I will not open you the windows of heaven, and pour you out a blessing, that there shall not be room enough to receive it" (Mal. 3:10).

The Awesome Declaration

Once again the word *if* was at the center of the divine message. God was more than willing to assist His people, but they were required to make the first move toward spiritual revival The bringing of the tithe to the altar of God was mandatory. This was not dependent upon the whims and fancies of people; it was the command of the Almighty. God's hands were seemingly tied until Israel removed all hindrances to the flow of blessings. It is interesting to remember that early in Jewish history the "windows of heaven" had been mentioned by an unbelieving nobleman who had scoffed at Elisha's prediction. He said, "Behold, if the LORD would make windows in heaven, might this thing be? (2 Kings 7:2). Since heaven is the home of the Almighty, He would not have difficulty opening one of His windows!

The Anointed Deliverer

"But unto you that fear my name shall the Sun of righteousness arise with healing in his wings; and ye shall go forth, and grow up as calves of the stall" (Mal. 4:2). "The calves of the stall" were protected and fed by a loving owner. During winter, when food was scarce, he cared for them; but when spring arrived and grass was growing in the fields, the door of the barn was opened, and the calves went out to frolic in the sunshine. The term "grow up" means "to frolic." Hence, the word in the Septuagint version of the Scriptures, *skipteesete*—Ye shall leap! God was trying to teach His people that nothing would be impossible. No blessing would be withheld if they would bring their tithes into the store house. When people rob God, they are already bankrupt! (see Mal. 3:8–9).

"And Jesus being full of the Holy Ghost, returned from Jordan, and was led by the Spirit into the wilderness, being forty days tempted of the devil. And in those days he did eat nothing: and when they were ended, he afterward hungered" (Luke 4:1–2).

Throughout His stay upon the earth, the Savior was permanently full of the Holy Spirit, and that explained two things: (1) His continuing victory over evil; and (2) Satan's never-ceasing assault upon Christ's holiness. The only assured method of living victoriously is to be completely possessed and controlled by God.

The Continuing Assault . . . *How Fierce*

When discussing the temptation of Christ, theologians draw attention to the three main suggestions made by Satan. Yet, it must be remembered the Savior had already endured forty days of unprecedented anguish. The details of that month-long struggle were never revealed, but it may be assumed the conflict was severe. Then, when the struggle had apparently ended, Satan attacked the physical weakness of Jesus. The Lord had been without a substantial meal for weeks, and fasting must have had an effect upon His physical condition. He needed nourishment, and since there was no store in the area, the Devil tried to trick Jesus into the sin of selfishness. He said, "If thou be the Son of God, command this stone that it be made bread" (4:3). It would not have been sinful to partake of legitimate food, but it would have been wrong to yield to any suggestion of the Devil. To place self-satisfaction before obedience to the laws of God would have been a mistake. Throughout temptations Satan's insinuations were false and misleading. He said, "If thou therefore wilt worship me, all shall be thine" (4:7). His nefarious suggestions questioned the authority and integrity of the Savior. Satan offers many attractive things, but the price is always too great to pay. He offered the prodigal son a glorious time in a foreign land, but the unfortunate young man ultimately stole pigs' food in order to survive. The Devil always takes away far more than he gives.

The Complete Answer . . . *How Faithful*

Each time Christ was tempted by the Devil, He prefaced His reply with the same statement, "It is written." It became increasingly evident that Jesus knew the Scriptures intimately and was determined not to do anything contrary to the will of His Father. Perhaps it was possible to give to Jesus all the kingdoms of the world; that is, Satan could have withdrawn opposition in every country. Apparently he was offering a shortcut to world domination. He suggested an easy way to give the Lord what He most desired. Yet Christ knew "the longest way around is the shortest way home!" The complete and final answer to temptation is conformity to the will of God.

The Commanding Assurance . . . *How Firm*

Many people are still deceived by the prince of evil. They believe his offers to be charming, alluring and satisfying. The subtle attractions of soft lights and sweet music have lured unsuspecting victims to their doom. It is wise to study carefully any person who suggests walking on thin ice! To change the image, it is better to build an insignificant cottage on solid rock, than to erect a glittering palace on shifting sand! The Lord was the Creator of the universe, but He also appreciated common sense! He came to earth, not as the Everlasting Father, but as a man subject to the laws of men. Had He jumped unwisely from the pinnacle of the temple, His body would have been broken by the rocks upon which He fell. That tragedy would have prevented the establishment of the kingdom of God. It was true that David had written, "For he shall give his angels charge over thee, to keep thee in all thy ways" (Ps. 91:11), but the angels were never commissioned to protect people whose actions were self-destructive. Some of the most attractive plants in the world emit poison. Contact with poison ivy can be dangerous, and the identical truth is evident with everything connected with Satan's attractive offers. They ruin happiness and destroy human souls.

Young people should be aware of the false promises of evil. Drugs offer the possibility of riding high but leave an addict in the lowest depths of suffering and shame. The praise and company of other addicts offer gaiety but leave the soul utterly lonely and desiring suicide. A fence at the top of a cliff is better than an ambulance at the bottom. The Bible says that Satan is a liar, and that conclusion is a fair assessment of his character. His offers are poison pills coated with sugar! The Lord knew this and acted accordingly.

"In the last day, that great day of the feast, Jesus stood and
cried, saying, If any man thirst let him come unto me, and drink.
He that believeth on me . . . out of his belly (inner man) shall
flow rivers of living water" (John 7:37–38).

The day was hot and sultry. The people in the crowded streets of Jerusalem were restless and terribly thirsty. The services in the temple had been long and demanding, and all the visitors were anticipating the opportunity to return to their distant homes. Suddenly a voice echoed down the street, "Are you thirsty?" That seemingly simple question astounded everybody. Water was almost unobtainable—throats remained dry and lips were parched. The cry was repeated with an invitation, "If any man thirst, let him come unto me and drink." When the listeners converged on a street corner, they saw Jesus, but He had no water skins from which they could drink. Doubtless some of the people were disappointed and critical, but many years later John explained that incident. He wrote, "But this spake he of the Spirit, which they that believe on him should receive" (John 7:39). Evidently it was only after a long period of time John and the other disciples understood the significance of Christ's statement.

The Great Requirement . . . *"If Any Man Thirst"*

This was not a momentary, emotional idea. They were thirsty. Their throats burned, and their tongues were dry. The dusty, desertlike conditions were appalling. They desperately needed to drink. David would have understood the situation, for he wrote, "As the hart panteth after the water brooks, so panteth my soul after thee, O God. My soul thirsteth for God, for the living God: when shall I come and appear before God? My tears have been my meat day and night" (Ps. 42:1–3). He had watched the graceful deer going to drink at the stream. When drought ravaged the land, he had seen their tongues protruding as if every fiber of their beings yearned for water. They seemed to be saying, "If we do not find water, we shall die!" Some religious people know little, if anything, of this desperate longing of the soul. Complacently, they remain content with an occasional Sunday morning visit to the church reservoir. The psalmist said, "Blessed are they that keep his testimonies, and that seek him with the whole heart" (Ps. 119:2).

The Glorious Response. . . . *"Let Him Come unto Me and Drink"*

"He that believeth (rests, depends) on me, out of his inmost being, shall flow rivers of living water." Many years later when John wrote his gospel, he realized the Savior was thinking of the world which resembled a desert. It desperately needed the living water, clear as crystal, which proceeds from the throne of God and of the Lamb (see Rev. 22:1). Yet water had to be conveyed through special channels. Only irrigation ditches could carry supplies to the places of need. John recognized that the living water from heaven would have to be carried by specially prepared people. Those channels would need to be consecrated men and women who depended upon the Savior. John knew such workers. He wrote of those who "for his name's sake . . . went forth, taking nothing of the Gentiles" (see 3 John 7).

The Gentle Rivers . . . *". . . Rivers of Living Water"*

At first Jesus invited people to drink, but there was a vast difference between a drink and a river! Perhaps He was urging them to drink often or indicating that His amazing power could transform little into much! Rivers must have a constant source of supply, or they will dry up. Even pools would evaporate in desert conditions at midday. The Lord was enunciating the simple fact that if His followers maintained a constant thirst for His fullness, unfailing resources would transform the wilderness into a garden through them.

Yet nothing would be accomplished unless the Master and His men worked together. If they would do their part, He would do His. Jesus appeared to be suggesting that unless His disciples drank often from God's supplies, they would have nothing to give to others. Unfortunately, all Christian workers know the feeling of resembling a squeezed-out orange! Pastors who have nothing left to give to their congregations, should re-establish contact with God's eternal fountain. It must never be forgotten that as barren earth awaits the arrival of life-giving rain, so men and women await the soul-refreshing gift which only God can supply. If we are to become His irrigation ditches, we should remove all debris from the channels. Ditches never clean out themselves!

MARTHA AND THE "IF" THAT OPENED
GOD'S TREASURY

"Jesus saith unto her, Said I not unto thee, that, if thou wouldest believe, thou shouldest see the glory of God?" (John 11:40).

The writer to the Hebrews expressed one of the greatest spiritual truths when he wrote, "But without faith it is impossible to please him: for he that cometh to God must believe that he is, and that he is a rewarder of them that diligently seek him" (Heb. 11:6). Faith is the key that unlocks the treasure house of heaven. God likes to be believed! Nevertheless, men forget this fact, and continually seek for visible evidence as a prelude to believing. It was significant that when the Savior reminded Martha, He said, "If thou wouldest believe, thou shouldest see the glory of God." Faith led to special blessings. Yet when the Lord was nailed to His cross, the chief priests said, "Let Christ the King of Israel descend now from the cross that we may see and believe" (Mark 15:32). Men seek signs; God desires faith, a faith which tenaciously clings to His promises.

The People Who Requested

"The Pharisees also with the Sadducees came, and tempting desired him that he would shew them a sign from heaven. He answered and said unto them, . . . A wicked and adulterous generation seeketh after a sign; and there shall no sign be given unto it, but the sign of the prophet Jonas" (Matt. 16:1–4). People asked the Lord to show them a sign from heaven when every day, He healed the sick and performed unprecedented miracles. The blind were being made to see; the lame walked; the lepers were cleansed, and the dead were being raised. Homes were transformed, and people were discovering Christ solved all kinds of problems.

Yet the Pharisees and Sadducees requested a sign from heaven. They were not blind. They chose not to see! Furthermore, had the Lord granted their desire, they would have repeated their request. They would not have been satisfied with one or two or any number of miracles. The petition would have been repeated daily. Human nature has not changed. The most effective way to fill an auditorium is to advertise healing services. People who seldom attend a religious service hurry to such meetings to see something sensational.

The Person Who Remembered

It is interesting to note that when Luke wrote about the rich man and Lazarus, he did not describe a parable! He wrote, "There was a certain rich man . . . ." Elsewhere the Lord's illustrations were cited as parables, but on this occasion Christ described something which had really happened. The Lord supplied a glimpse into the hereafter when He mentioned a rich man who had been unable to take his wealth into eternity. When that person discovered there was no comfort beyond the grave, he made a request that Lazarus be sent to earth to warn his brothers, "Lest they also come into this place of torment. Abraham saith unto him, They have Moses and the prophets; let them hear them. And he said, Nay, father Abraham: but if one went unto them from the dead, they will repent. And he said unto him, If they hear not Moses and the prophets, neither will they be persuaded though one rose from the dead" (Luke 16:28–31). Evidently the deceased man still believed signs were more necessary than faith.

The Preacher Who Rejected

It was sad that Thomas, who knew so much, understood so little! He had traversed the highways and byways of Palestine announcing the kingdom of God was at hand. He had followed his Master for three years, but faith did not occupy a central place in his life. When he heard of the resurrection of the Lord, he said, "Except I shall see in his hands the print of the nails, and put my finger into the print of the nails, and thrust my hand into his side, I will not believe" (John 20:25). Later, "Jesus saith unto him, Thomas, because thou hast seen me, thou hast believed; blessed are they that have not seen, and yet have believed" (20:29). "Now faith is the substance of things hoped for; the evidence of things not seen" (Heb. 11:1).

"And [Jesus] said unto them, Why are ye so fearful? How is it that ye have no faith? (Mark 4:40). "And He saith unto them, Why are ye fearful? O ye of little faith" (Matt. 8:26). "I have not found so great faith, no, not in Israel" (Matt. 8:10).

> Simply trusting every day,
> Trusting through a stormy way:
> Even when my faith is small,
> Trusting Jesus, that is all.

"I am the vine, ye are the branches: He that abideth in me, and I in him, the same bringeth forth much fruit: for without me ye can do nothing, . . . If ye abide in me, and my words abide in you, ye shall ask what ye will, and it shall be done unto you" (John 15:5, 7).

Apart from special circumstances, fruit must be cultivated, and the greatness of the harvest is commensurate with the amount of effort expended by the cultivator. Crops can easily be ruined, and wise farmers are familiar with certain indispensable conditions. The Lord had this thought in mind when He mentioned His *if* of fruitbearing. It was significant that He spoke of fruit, more fruit, and much fruit. All the stages of fruitbearing were dependent upon the conditional word *if.*

The Indisputable Productivity

A fruitless Christian is a person who never produces the characteristics mentioned by Paul (see Gal. 5:22–23). Fruitlessness may be caused by several things: (1) *An unused fertilizer.* Fertilizers left in the barn never improve unproductive soil. Similarly, the rich provision made by the Lord is useless unless individuals appropriate it to themselves. All Christians should desire to bring forth a harvest for the glory of God; (2) *An unrelenting freeze.* The lack of rain or very low temperatures can ruin any harvest. If a man or woman permits the soul to become frigid and cold, spiritual fruitbearing becomes impossible; (3) *An unchallenged foe.* If the Mediterranean fruit flies had been permitted to remain in California, economic disaster would have paralyzed the state. When enemies attack the soul, every effort must be made to exterminate them; (4) *An unwise farmer.* Solomon wrote, "I went by the field of the slothful . . . and lo, it was all grown over with thorns . . . . Then I saw, and considered it well . . . Yet a little sleep, a little slumber, a little folding of the hands to sleep; so shall thy poverty come" (Prov. 24:30–34). To avoid these calamities, men must abide in Christ that His life can flow through the human branches.

The Inspired Prayer

The Lord said, "*If* ye abide in me, and my words abide in you, ye shall ask what ye will, and it shall be done unto you" (John 15:7). The initial word *if* indicates answers to prayer are conditional upon a believer abiding in Christ. If a person does not do this, he or she has no right to expect affirmative responses to a petition. James wrote, "Ye ask, and receive not, because ye ask amiss, that ye may consume it upon your lusts" (James 4:3). Prayers can be selfishly motivated. Every prayer of Jesus was answered for He never sought anything which was wrong. Increased fruitbearing is only possible when Christians abide in the will of God. The flow of sap from the parent tree must be unhindered; otherwise, the fruit will be undeveloped, tasteless, small and unsatisfying.

The Increased Pleasure

The Lord said, "If ye keep my commandments, ye shall abide in my love; even as I have kept my Father's commandments, and abide in his love. These things have I spoken unto you, that my joy might remain in you, and that your joy might be full" (John 15:10–11). These marvelous utterances were preceded by that conditional conjunction *if*. If we abide in Christ, we bear fruit. If we abide in Him, we receive answers to prayer. If we abide in Him, our happiness increases, and our "joy will be full." The Christian who does not abide in Christ is like a stunted tree, a useless piece of timber, a blight in an orchard, and a disappointment to its owner. People whose petitions are not granted never experience the joy of seeing miracles; inspiration never thrills their souls.

The psalmist described such people when he wrote, "By the rivers of Babylon, there we sat down, yea, we wept, when we remembered Zion. We hanged our harps upon the willows in the midst thereof. For there they that carried us away captive required of us mirth, saying, Sing us one of the songs of Zion. How shall we sing the Lord's song in a strange land?" (see Ps. 137:1–4). People who do not abide in the will of God live in a Babylon of their own creation. A man who is not helpful to his Master is haunted by his memories! Babylonian fruit could never be compared with the fruit of the Hebrew homeland. It is better to be inspired by abiding in Christ than to just exist in any other place.

JAMES AND HIS "IF" OF HEALING
AND FORGIVENESS

"Is any sick among you? let him call for the elders of the church; and let them pray over him, anointing him with oil in the name of the Lord: And the prayer of faith shall save the sick, and the Lord shall raise him up; and if he have committed sins, they shall be forgiven him" (James 5:14–15).

This is one of the most challenging statements in the New Testament. James was the chairman of the Jerusalem elders, and matters of jurisprudence were referred to him. Occasionally, he was required to solve problems which affected all the churches. The word *if* occupied a central part in this Scripture and was used to differentiate between the healing of the body and the forgiveness of the soul. During the history of the church leaders disagreed and assemblies were divided. Sometimes calm consideration yields better results than emotional debates.

Proposition One . . . *Sickness Is Not Always the Result of Secret Sin*

All sickness is the result of Adam's sin, but to suggest illness is evidence of a person's secret guilt is erroneous. Sometimes this has been true. For example, four men brought their friend to Jesus in quest of healing. The Lord dealt with the sickness in the soul and then healed the man's body (see Luke 5:18–26). Yet, this could not have been the reason for the illness of Trophimus whom Paul left at Melitum (see 2 Tim. 4:20). The apostle who often healed the sick could have handled that situation immediately. Probably the man needed rest, but the only way to supply this was to put him in bed! James supplied guidance for many churches and in connection with the healing of the sick, said: "*If* he have committed sins, they shall be forgiven him."

Proposition Two . . . *The Text Cannot Mean What Some Teachers Claim*

The apostle suggested that any sick person should share his problem with the elders of the local church who would reciprocate by anointing the sufferer with oil; their prayer of faith would provide a miracle. It should never be forgotten that this advice is still relevant. God can, and does heal the sick. Nevertheless, that promise is not a blank check on the bank of God's sufficiency. All healing is subject to the will of God. When people *demand* that God heal the sick, they are either over-confident or arrogant. If God must do as He is requested, then Christians would never need a doctor nor an undertaker. They should be able at any age—fifty, sixty, or even a hundred years—to do as James suggested, and healing would be instantaneous. Christians would live forever as long as the elders of the church responded to their requests!

The arrogant person bays, "Lord, You must heal me!" The humble person says, "Lord, I know You can do it, but I am not worthy that You should." The person of faith says, "Lord, I am trusting to find favor in Thy sight. Yet, not my will but Thine be done. If it will please Thee, heal my body." "And the prayer of faith shall save the sick, and the Lord shall raise him up."

Proposition Three . . . *A Man May Be Sick in Several Ways*

It is possible to be sick in soul, body, and mind. A body may be wracked with pain, a soul tormented by guilt, or a mind partially or completely deranged. James would agree that healing covered every area of human experience. God can and does heal sick bodies; He certainly saves the soul, and fills the mind with peace beyond understanding. Nevertheless, that kind of faith is found only in humble souls who never *demand* responses from the "giver of every good and perfect gift." They prefer, reverently, to seek His gracious cooperation. If and when, for reasons best known to Himself, God temporarily withholds assistance, true faith never seeks someone to blame for the resulting disappointment.

Many years ago I met a young Christian who was seriously ill, but she never requested other Christians to anoint her body with oil nor pray for her physical recovery. She had no desire to be healed. She loved her Savior immensely and desperately desired to be in His presence. "For [she] looked for a city which hath foundations, whose builder and maker is God" (Heb. 11:10). At that time I was a young pastor and serving the Lord was of paramount importance to me. Why anyone should desire to die was completely beyond my comprehension. Now I know what that young lady and Paul believed. "For I am in a strait betwixt two, having a desire to depart, and to be with Christ; which is far better" (Phil. 1:23).

PETER AND HIS "IF" OF A RESPLENDENT
HOME-GOING

*"For if ye do these things, ye shall never fall: For so an entrance
shall be ministered unto you abundantly into the everlasting
kingdom of our Lord and Savior Jesus Christ" (2 Peter 1:10–11).*

Simon Peter had strong convictions! He believed a man's faith
would provide an entrance into heaven, but only conformity to the
will of God could provide *an abundant entrance.* During my stay in
Melbourne, Australia, I stood on a high vantage point and watched
the homecoming parade of soldiers who had survived a terrible
ambush in the Korean War. They were all that remained of the First
Australian Division which went to fight in that conflict. I was unaware of what was taking place until a stranger said, "What is left of
that company came home last night, and in a few minutes they will
place a wreath on the national cenotaph. They will do this in memory of their comrades who did not come home. We are here to give
them a great welcome."

I was enthralled as I watched the proceedings. First came the
police motorcyclists to make sure the street was cleared of traffic;
then came the mounted police on their magnificent horses, and after
the military band came those gallant men. Suddenly, pandemonium
broke loose as hundreds of young women ran to the marching
soldiers to kiss and hug them while the immense crowd continued
to cheer. The men had performed valiantly on the field of battle,
and were receiving *an abundant welcome* into their homeland.

As a vivid contrast, I remembered my entry into Australia when
an ill-tempered customs officer temporarily made my life a misery.
He made me open all my luggage and asked all kinds of questions.
When he had finished the examination, I felt extremely fortunate
even to set foot in the country. Peter would have understood!

Continually Striving . . . *To Improve*

Peter thought there was always room for improvement. He believed that however close to his Master a Christian might be, it was
always possible to get closer. Peter would have made a great collec-
tor of precious things; he was always adding to what he possessed.
He began with faith in the precious blood of Christ but then went on
to deeper experiences. He wrote of adding virtue, knowledge, tem-
perance, patience, godliness, brotherly love, kindness, and charity

(see 2 Peter 1:5–7). It would be easy to visualize his meeting with people camped on the lower elevations of God's mountain of grace. Having heard their testimony, he would urge them to break camp and renew their climb toward the summit. Grace leads to godliness; happiness should forerun holiness, and salvation should be an introduction to service. These were lessons to be learned prior to graduation in God's academy. Peter emphasized these facts, saying, "If ye do these things, ye shall never fall." He was not content to see men and women enlisting in the army of the Lord; he wanted them to be enrolled in the Officers' Training Company! Those who had been taught by others should prepare to instruct new recruits. Promotion was not automatic; it had to be earned.

Constant Safety . . . *Never Falling*

Peter never forgot that he had denied his Lord, but he knew that could not have happened if he had done what he was now recommending to his readers. He had not given much attention to what the Lord had spoken, and his negligence nearly ruined his soul. "Ye shall never fall" meant the climber had reached a higher altitude where he was in good company for his heavenly guide was also on that plateau. The recruit had become a seasoned veteran. The Commander in Chief had seen and approved of His soldier. The joy of complete victory was already thrilling the soul of the aspiring Christian. His medal of merit was already assigned—even before the journey was completed.

Complete Serenity . . . *An Abundant Entrance*

That Peter prefaced his message with the conditional *if* signified not every soldier would become a general! An abundant entrance into the homeland depended on the quality of service rendered on the battlefields of earth. Every soldier would reach the eternal city, but some would arrive almost unnoticed! All would be able to respond when "the roll is called up yonder," but not everyone would be called to the front of the assembled witnesses to be awarded the medal of honor and listen to the plaudits of angelic hosts. Peter emphasized that such a celebration would only be known if the readers of his epistle did what he advised. "If ye do these things," the final result will be assured. Christians should aim high! If they shot at a tree, they would hit their target. If they aimed at the sky, they might even surprise themselves!

*"But if we walk in the light, as he is in the light, we have
fellowship one with another, and the blood of Jesus Christ
his Son cleanseth us from all sin" (1 John 1:7).*

It is believed that John lived to be over ninety years of age and
during his lifetime saw many changes within the church. False teachers had assumed leadership. Their arrogance was unpardonable, and
their doctrines were contrary to the teachings of the Savior. They
said that since the death of Jesus obtained unconditional pardon for
the sinner, human responsibility had terminated; believers could do
as they pleased! There was no need to worry about anything; the
blood of Christ had obtained unlimited freedom for mankind. They
taught that since eternal life could never be lost, sin was no longer a
threat. There was no need for doctrines of holiness. John rebuked
this heresy and sent ripples of apprehension throughout the assemblies.

The "If" of Folly

"If we say that we have fellowship with him, and walk in darkness, we lie, and do not the truth" (1 John 1:6). "If we say that we
have no sin, we deceive ourselves, and the truth is not in us" (1 John
1:8). "If we say that we have not sinned, we make him a liar, and
his word is not in us" (1 John 1:10). John used the conditional word
if six times in as many verses. Evidently, he believed deeds were
more important than declarations. What a man *was* superseded anything he uttered. Unless testimony were based upon the Word of
God, profession was an empty shell, a house built on shifting sand.
That was folly of the greatest magnitude which placed the sinner in
danger.

The "If" of Fellowship

John spoke of fellowship, but the text might have a two-fold interpretation. It is possible to fellowship with God and with others who
share that delightful experience. It is the best cure for loneliness, but
John insisted the privilege was conditional. Two men may walk together and argue every step of their journey. That is not fellowship. People
may converse on the telephone, but that also is hardly fellowship. A
telephone conversation can never be an effective substitute for the
beholding of a loved one's face—the warmth of an embrace and the

sharing of the love and respect one has for the other. True fellowship means meeting, giving, and sharing. These treasures should be known by all Christians; they are the spiritual cement which binds together the living stones in the temple of God. As the original disciples walked and talked with their Lord, other believers could know that experience. Through the presence of the Holy Spirit, Christ was still among His people. Nevertheless, unless they walked with Him, fellowship was only a word in their vocabulary!

The "If" of Forgiveness

This was the most trenchant of John's statements. He wrote, "But if we walk in the light, as he is in the light, . . . the blood of Jesus Christ his Son cleanseth us from all sin" (see 1 John 1:7). The word "cleanseth" is a translation of the Greek word *katharizei* and is a special word expressing the continuous tense of the verb. It literally means, "to go on cleansing." All this is conditional on the word *if*. The precious blood of Christ does not go on cleansing the Christian unless his confession is followed by walking in the light. Some people ask for pardon, then they return to their sinning as quickly as possible. Does that kind of prayer restore peace to the human soul? If a person is a true Christian, can he or she disregard the commandments of God? A man should never expect forgiveness unless he learns to detest that which defiles his soul.

No ordinance of the church or words of a priest or pastor can be of worth unless a person is determined to "walk in the light as Chrsit is in the light." There is a vast difference between sinning and loving sin. Lot lived in Sodom and had no intention of leaving that city. It was only the grace of God which brought him out. When a person surrenders to God, he receives an unconditional pardon; but that is not a license to continue evil ways. When God gives us a clean soul, it becomes our responsibility to keep it clean! When Christ brings us out of the prison of guilt and shame, we should never voluntarily return to its shadows. People who do return cannot appreciate the gravity of evil or the atoning worth of the Savior's death.

> Lord Jesus Christ, grow Thou in me,
> And all things else recede.
> My heart be daily nearer Thee,
> From sin be daily freed.

"Behold, I stand at the door and knock: if any man hear my voice, and open the door, I will come in to him, and will sup with him, and he with me" (Rev. 3:20).

If modern terms may be used to describe the church in Laodicea, it might be described as the pride of its members and the delight of the denomination to which it belonged. Its tall, tapering steeple would be seen from great distances, its ornate frontispiece would be displaying elegance, and the parking lot would be filled with Continentals and Cadillacs! All the members would be citizens of note, occupying positions of trust and eminence. The minister would possess the highest academic distinction, and the choir would be filled with professional singers. Everything money could buy would be evident throughout the beautiful building. Yet in the narthex would be a missionary box, and over its coin slot would be a thick cobweb! An artist painted such a picture, and depicted the Savior, hand poised in mid-air, about to seek admittance. When the Lord sent a letter to that church, He reminded the members that in spite of His disappointment, He still sought an entrance. *If* a person would open the door—so it must have been closed—He would be delighted to accept an invitation to dine.

A Closed Door That Might Have Been Opened (Genesis 7:16)

The ancient world had never known such excitement; it seemed a circus had arrived in town! Unattended animals had been converging on a district where a strange old man had built the world's first ship. It was all so confusing, but the situation was hilarious! The sound of hammers and saws had long since become part of the daily routine. The noise only ceased when the master carpenter became a preacher. This type of thing had continued for one hundred and twenty years, and the people were a little tired of the same sermon. Noah insisted that a great flood was coming, that he would not need to move his vessel to a beach. That pesky old preacher was annoying his audience, for he had become a meddler! When he denounced their illicit conduct, they were incensed. But he was old and harmless, and at least his animals were interesting.

Then events suddenly changed. The ship was completed, and Noah began loading his freight. It was so funny, for that ship was going nowhere! The neighbors watched Noah and his family going aboard and probably wished him *bon voyage*. It was surprising when the great door closed of its own accord! "And they that went in, went in male and female of all flesh, as God had commanded him; and the Lord shut him in" (Gen. 7:16). The Bible says, "And it came to pass after seven days, that the waters of the flood were upon the earth" (Gen. 7:10). Why did God wait a week when the ship was ready to begin its journey? The answer may be expressed in one word—grace—for if any man had knocked in faith upon that door, he would have been admitted.

A *Closed Door That Never Opened* (Matthew 25:10)

The Lord was a great preacher; when He described scenes, His word pictures were vivid. Ten young ladies attending a wedding had decided, according to the custom of the times, to go forth to welcome the bridegroom. They were determined to have a great time. Yet something had delayed the husband-to-be. They were very tired, and one of their number suggested they should sleep for a short time and take advantage of the delay. "And at midnight there was a cry made, Behold, the bridegroom cometh; go ye out to meet him" (Matt. 25:6). Then came problems! Five of the young women had forgotten to bring oil in their containers, and they were desperate. At that late hour the shops would be closed. They would have to awaken a trader! "And while they went to buy, the bridegroom came, and they that were ready went in with him to the marriage: and the door was shut" (Matt. 25:10). That door was never reopened, at least not to them.

A *Closed Door That Should Have Been Opened* (Revelation 3:20)

Perhaps the minister and his elders were unaware that Jesus was seeking admittance. He who had been on the inside inviting people to enter, was now on the outside. If the people knew this, they could not have cared less. A voice was saying "*If* any man will open the door, I will come in to him, and will sup with him, and he with me." They shrugged their shoulders. Who could be bothered with the Man in the street when they were enjoying themselves? Did they ever open that door? If not, it would have been the third occurrence of its type in the Scriptures.

*"Be thou faithful unto death, and I will give thee
a crown of life" (Rev. 2:10).*

This is an age of drop outs, and students are constantly reminded
that unless they continue their studies they have no future in modern
society. Within the early church the same kind of failure caused
concern. Many professing Christians lost their enthusiasm and
stopped serving Christ. Persecution, indifference, and other attractions caused this breakdown, and ultimately John was commissioned to send messages to the churches in Asia. It was significant
that at the conclusion of each of the seven letters, Christ urged His
readers to persevere to the end, to resist becoming a drop out! He
mentioned rewards for overcomers and emphasized that those who
failed to continue in God's service would have no chance of fame in
the kingdom of God. That message is relevant today.

The First Promise . . . A *Special Privilege* (Revelation 2:7)

"To him that overcometh will I give to eat of the tree of life."
The tree of life was first mentioned in Genesis 3:22 where it was
meant to be the channel through which Adam and Eve could have
become immortal. They lost their opportunity and eventually died
as sinners. The same tree is mentioned in Revelation 22:2 where its
leaves will supply healing for the nations. Since there will be no sin
in the eternal ages, the tree of life signifies the way by which mortal
beings gain immortality. This special privilege indicates the greatness of God's salvation. "Death is swallowed up in victory" (1 Cor.
15:54).

The Second Promise . . . A *Special Protection* (Revelation 2:11)

"He that overcometh shall not be hurt of the second death."
Obtaining everlasting life is a great experience, but the promise that
it will never be threatened again is greater. At the end of time the
dead will appear before the throne of God, and "they were judged
every man according to their works. And death and hell were cast
into the lake of fire. This is the second death" (Rev. 20:13–14).

The Third Promise . . . A *Special Provision* (Revelation 2:17)

The text may have connections with the manna stored in the ark
of the covenant and with the statement made by Christ, "I am that

bread of life" (John 6:48). The "white stone" signifies the welcome given into God's country (see the author's book, *Bible Treasures*, page 161).

The Fourth Promise . . . *A Special Power* (Revelation 2:26)

"And he that overcometh, and keepeth my works unto the end, to him will I give power over the nations." To exercise authority over nations suggests a special position occupied by God's favored people. It might refer to positions of eminence in our present world, but is more likely a reference to the time when saints reign with Christ. Everlasting life assures believers of a place within the kingdom; the reward of power indicates their importance within that kingdom.

The Fifth Promise . . . *A Special Profession* (Revelation 3:5)

Once again the Lord gave a threefold promise. His faithful servants would be clothed in righteousness; their name will never be erased from the Book of Life; and best of all, they will be honored before God and angels. It would be significant to be recognized by any king or queen, yet, that would fade into insignificance when compared with the recognition promised by the King of Kings.

The Sixth Promise . . . *A Special Pillar* (Revelation 3:12)

This utterance indicates tremendous importance within the New Jerusalem, the city which will descend from heaven. The Lord will be thrilled to be identified with His faithful servants. This means fellowship of the best kind. "Him that overcometh will I make a pillar in the temple of my God . . . I will write upon him my new name."

The Seventh Promise . . . *A Special Place* (Revelation 3:21)

"To him that overcometh will I grant to sit with me in my throne." This was the last of seven rewards promised to those who became overcomers. It is impossible to assess the loss of drop outs. Writing to the Galatians, Paul said, "O foolish Galatians, who hath bewitched you? . . . Ye did run well; who did hinder you?" (Gal. 3:1; 5:7). At the end of his life on earth, the apostle was abe to write, "I have fought a good fight, I have finished my course, I have kept the faith: Henceforth there is laid up for me a crown" (2 Tim. 4:7–8). Every Christian should be able to give an identical testimony when he goes to meet the Lord.

Unconditional Promises

ABRAHAM WHO MADE AN
UNQUALIFIED COMMITMENT

*"And Abraham said unto his young men, Abide ye here
with the ass; and I and the lad will go yonder and
worship, and will come again to you" (Gen. 22:5).*

Abraham was deep in thought; he was facing the greatest crisis
of his life. He had been instructed by the Lord to offer Isaac as a
sacrifice upon Mount Moriah, but the more he considered the command, the greater became his problem. Nothing made sense! Isaac,
his beloved son, had become the center around which life revolved
and upon whom the future depended. The boy's presence made life
worthwhile; he was his mother's pride and joy. The thought of
offering him as a sacrifice was totally obnoxious and senseless. Yet
God had commanded this, and Abraham was obliged to make a
choice: either to do as commanded or to refuse cooperation with the
Lord. He was at an impasse.

A Test of His Feelings

Obviously, he had to decide who came first in his affections—
God or Isaac. There were various ways to consider the problem. If
he refused to obey God, then Isaac could die just as easily as he had
been born. His birth had been a miracle, but his decease could be
swift. In that event, having disobeyed God, Abraham would be left
alone. He loved his son immensely, but nothing could change the
fact he loved the Lord even more. God's command had shocked
him, for it was unnatural to expect a father to kill his only child;
when Abraham reflected on the matter, his conclusion was inevitable. The Lord was not foolish; there had to be a reason for His
command. "And Abraham rose up early in the morning, and sad-
dled his ass, and took two of his young men with him, and Isaac his
son, and clave the wood for the burnt offering, and rose up, and
went unto the place of which God had told him" (Gen. 22:3).

A Test of His Faith

During that journey he had time to reflect. He remembered
the domestic strife between Sarah, his wife, and Hagar, the servant. At that time God had said, "In all that Sarah hath said unto
thee, hearken unto her voice; for in Isaac shall thy seed be called"
(Gen. 21:12). The old man seemed to be in a trance! His thoughts

continued, "How can my seed be multiplied in Isaac if he dies as a child? Even the Lord cannot raise children from a corpse! Yet God cannot lie. Nothing seems to make sense, but if God is to bless and honor my name through Isaac, even though the lad be offered in sacrifice, it will be incumbent upon the Lord to restore his life." When Abraham reached the place where his servants were to remain, his problem had been solved. He told them to wait, and promised that when their mission had been completed, he and his son would return. That was a special promise, for at that moment he believed Isaac would be slain. Centuries later it was written, "By faith, Abraham, when he was tried, offered up Isaac: and he that had received the promises offered up his only begotten son, Of whom it was said, That in Isaac shall thy seed be called: Accounting that God was able to raise him up, even from the dead; from whence also he received him in a figure" (Heb. 11:17–19). That father never hesitated to take the knife; he knew that Isaac, even if he were slain, would be raised from the dead; otherwise the Lord would be a liar.

A Test of His Fellowship

Abraham was already a son of God by the creative process, but he became known as "the friend of God" (see James 2:23, and 2 Chron. 20:7). Which was the more valuable relationship—to be a child of God or His close friend? A son is related by nature to his parent, but fellowship between parent and child can sometimes be ruined. Close friends are seldom separated except by distance; each desires and enjoys the company of the other. There was never strain between God and His intimate friend. Perhaps there were times when Abraham found it difficult to understand why the Lord took a certain course of action, but when faith was tested, trust remembered God's promises. If it were possible to see Abraham's face when he took the knife to slay his son, the picture would be informative. Expectancy shone in the eyes of the old man; he never thought of blood streaming from a wound but considered only the power of resurrection raising his boy. He carried a knife but not a shovel! There would be no need to dig a grave; the boy would still be alive!

The promises of God are lifelines in stormy seas, a sure foundation upon which to build, a safe and true guide when life's highways are obscured by fog! God has never broken a promise; to rely upon His faithfulness is to exhibit wisdom.

THE PROMISE THAT HELPED
JOSHUA FILL BIG SHOES

*"There shall not any man be able to stand before thee
all the days of thy life; as I was with Moses, so I will be
with thee: I will not fail thee, nor forsake thee" (Josh. 1:5).*

To follow in the footsteps of Moses and become the new leader of Israel was not an easy task. The patriarch had spent forty years studying the military prowess of Pharaoh's army and another forty years exercising the patience and ability of a shepherd in the wilderness. He needed eighty years of intensive training before he became the leader of God's difficult people. They had been ungrateful, unworthy, and unsurpassed in their criticism, and it remained a mystery how Moses tolerated the people who made his life a misery. The patriarch had been an intimate friend of the Lord, but the time had arrived for another man to lead the nation. Joshua had been chosen by God to lead Israel into the Promised Land, and, to his everlasting credit it can be said he did a magnificent job.

An Unfailing God . . . *A Command to Serve*

Joshua received special training for his assignment. Nearly forty years earlier he had been one of the spies sent to gain information about the Promised Land, and he probably had vivid recollections of that eventful journey. It is believed by theologians that as a slave in Egypt, he was trained in Pharaoh's army and was later responsible for organizing a troup of slaves into a disciplined group of warriors. When Moses prayed for help to overcome the Amalekites, Joshua led Israel against the enemy. Afterward, God instructed the patriarch to ordain publicly his chief minister, so the entire nation would be aware of the authority bestowed upon the new leader (see Num. 27:18–23).

Joshua was a seasoned warrior, an able administrator, and a saint filled with the Holy Spirit. When God commanded him to take Israel into Canaan, he was ready for the gigantic task It was significant that the command, "Be strong and of a good courage" was given three times, and each had special significance. Joshua was urged to be strong for the sake of the land, the law, and the Lord. The reason for his bravery would be the abiding presence of the Lord. He would never be alone. The same promises can be claimed by every Christian worker who has a Canaan to conquer.

An Unwavering Guide . . . *A Challenge to Succeed*

"This book of the Law shall not depart out of thy mouth; but thou shalt meditate therein day and night, that thou mayest observe to do according to all that is written therein: for then thou shalt make thy way prosperous, and then thou shalt have good success" (Josh. 1:8). Evidently, Moses had committed to writing all that the Lord told him on the mountain. Joshua was present when God met with Moses, but a written record of what transpired would prevent forgetfulness. God had spoken, and He meant what He said! Without the strength of God's abiding presence, even the greatest military effort would fail. To govern and inspire the nation, Joshua would be asked to overcome innumerable difficulties. Civil and judicial problems would require attention; judgments would have to be made. Whatever was decided, some critics would complain of harsh treatment. Some of the people had been hostile toward Moses; they had not changed! The Scriptures were to be an infallible guide to the man who would read them daily.

An Unseen General . . . *A Companion to Share*

"And it came to pass, when Joshua was by Jericho . . . there stood a man over against him with his drawn sword in his hand: and Joshua went unto him, and said unto him, Art thou for us, or for our adversaries? And he said, Nay, but as captain of the host of the LORD am I now come . . . And the captain of the LORD's host said unto Joshua, Loose thy shoe from off thy foot; for the place whereon thou standest is holy. And Joshua did so" (Josh. 5:13–15). It was not permitted in Israel to worship any god but the Lord. Even angels rebuked those who mistakenly fell at their feet (see Rev. 22:8–9).

The fact that Joshua was permitted to worship and instructed to remove his sandal indicates that the Lord Jesus had come to earth to be the commander-in-chief of Israel's army. God never sent His servant to fight alone; He delighted in sharing the joys and problems of His people. As the eternal Word came to be with Joshua, so the Holy Spirit came at Pentecost to reside with and in Christians. The Captain of God's host was never seen again, but that was of no consequence. Joshua knew when the Lord was near—he knew His voice!

"And Joshua said, Hereby ye shall know that the living God is among you . . . it shall come to pass, as soon as the soles of the feet of the priests that bear the ark of the LORD, the Lord of all the earth, shall rest in the waters of Jordan, that the waters of Jordan shall be cut off from the waters that come down from above; and they shall stand upon an heap" (Josh. 3:10–13).

This obscure story in the book of Joshua has become one of the most challenged of all the Bible incidents. It describes how the waters of the flooded Jordan river were held back to provide a safe and dry crossing as the children of Israel entered Canaan. Theologians disagree in their interpretation of the account. Some deny its accuracy, stating it never happened. Others supply details suggesting the phenomenon was caused by an earthquake. Christians believe it was a miracle, the fulfillment of a very important promise.

The Significant Promise . . . *Illustrated*

It should be remembered that on that significant day much more was at stake than the crossing of a river. A new leader had arrived to take charge of the nation, and inevitably, some people would challenge his authority. Believing Moses was the ultimate in statemanship, they would be reluctant to obey his successor. God had said, "As I was with Moses, so will I be with thee," but something more was needed. Israel had to be convinced that God meant what He said. The crossing of the Jordan was the first test to be undertaken. When the Hebrews left Egypt, God assisted the Exodus by dividing the Red Sea (see Ex. 14:21–22). If God were to fulfill the promise made to Joshua, then it would be necessary to repeat His action. When the children of Israel saw the miraculous drying of the river, they remembered what God had promised, and their respect for Joshua increased.

The Special Power . . . *Influencing*

"The waters which came down from above stood and rose up upon an heap very far from the city of Adam, that is beside Zaretan: and those that came down toward the sea of the plain, even the salt sea, failed, and were cut off: and the people passed over right against Jericho" (Josh. 3:16). How could this sensational event occur? Many insist that this was no miracle since the event can be explained as a natural phenomenon. They point out that on December 8, 1267, an earthquake caused the high banks of the Jordan to collapse near Tell ed-Damiyeh, damming the river for about 10 hours. On July 11, 1927, another earthquake near the same location blocked the river for 21 hours. Of course these stoppages did not occur during flood season. Admittedly, God could have employed natural causes such as an earthquake and a landslide, but the timing would have still made it a miraculous intervention. Does the biblical text allow for such an interpretation of this event? Considering all the factors involved, it seems best to view this occurrence as a "special act of God brought about in a way unknown to man" (*The Bible Knowledge Commentary on the Old Testament,* p. 335, Walvoord and Zuck, Victor Books). Joshua said the event took place when the river Jordan was overflowing its banks. Only a cataclysmic event could have held back raging flood waters, and this became obvious to the people who might have discredited Joshua's authority.

The Stony Pillars . . . *Indicating*

The priests who walked by faith into the river were to be commended for their action. Men of lesser stature might have feared death by drowning. Nothing happened until the feet of the priests were actually in the water. "And as . . . the feet of the priests . . . were dipped in the brim of the water . . . that the waters which came down from above, stood and rose up upon an heap" (Josh. 3:15,16). "Faith is the substance of things hoped for, the evidence of things not seen" (Heb. 11:1). It is the key which unlocks the treasure house of heaven. The ten lepers cleansed by the Savior only experienced deliverance when they also walked by faith. "And it came to pass, that, as they went, they were cleansed" (Luke 17:14). Joshua erected two memorial pillars of stone, one in the bed of the river and the other on its bank. They were meant to remind the people they were leaving a carnal wilderness experience to seek a new, triumphant life in God's land of milk and honey.

> Got any rivers you think are uncrossable?
> Got any mountains you can't tunnel through?
> God specializes in things thought impossible;
> He can do things no other can do.

*"According to all these words, and according to all this vision,
so did Nathan speak to David. Then went king David in,
and sat before the LORD" (2 Sam. 7:17–18).*

The palace on Mount Zion had been completed; Jerusalem was at rest and David was dreaming. When he toured his luxurious home, his heart filled with pride, but his conscience was troubled. He compared his magnificent house with the inconspicuous tent in which the ark of the covenant resided and regretted that he lived in splendor when God was behind curtains! The more he considered the problem, the greater became his determination. He would build a temple for the Lord, and it would be the greatest structure in the world! When he shared his thoughts with Nathan, the prophet was delighted and said, "Go, do all that is in thine heart; for the LORD is with thee" (2 Sam. 7:3). That night sleep was elusive; David lay awake planning how to complete his task. The temple would be vast in extent, exceedingly beautiful, and even the Lord would be proud of it. But David's dreams were never realized; the Lord had different ideas.

Sitting Before the Lord . . . *A Cure for Great Disappointment*

"And it came to pass that night that the word of the LORD came unto Nathan, saying, Go and tell my servant David, Thus saith the Lord . . . when thy days be fulfilled, and thou shalt sleep with thy fathers, I will set up thy seed after thee . . . and I will establish his kingdom. He shall build an house for my name, and I will stablish the throne of his kingdom for ever" (2 Sam. 7:4–5, 12–13). Further information was supplied later. "And David said to Solomon, My son, as for me, it was in my mind to build an house unto the name of the LORD my God; But, the word of the LORD came to me, saying . . . thou hast shed much blood upon the earth in my sight. Behold a son shall be born to thee . . . He shall build an house for my name" (1 Chron. 22:7–10). When disappointment fills the heart and chills the spirit, it is wise to sit at God's feet.

Sitting Before the Lord . . . *A Call for Growing Determination*

David desired to build a house for God; the Lord planned to build a house for David. The king's disappointment began to diminish as he contemplated the details of God's message. His pouting was replaced by praise when he considered he would be given a son whose kingdom would never be destroyed. It is debatable whether David understood the implications of that great utterance, for evidently it would not be fulfilled during the lifetime of Solomon. The Davidic kingdom would last until the Messiah sat upon the throne of Israel. Suddenly, David smiled and made a vow. If he could not build the temple, he would prepare materials to assist his son who would do it for him. "And David said, Solomon my son is young and tender, and the house that is to be builded for the LORD must be exceeding magnifical, of fame and of glory throughout all countries. I will therefore now make preparation for it. So David prepared abundantly before his death" (1 Chron. 22:5). The king's cooperation became an asset of incalculable worth when Solomon began his reign. It was refreshing that God's blessing was more to be desired than anything else in the world. Many people who cannot be leaders in a project or the kingdom resign their position and withdraw. They prove they are smaller than the thing which upset them.

Sitting Before the Lord . . . *A Cause for Glorious Devotion*

"Then went David in and sat before the LORD . . . ." He probably knelt in the sanctuary and sat back on his heels. From that position it was easy to lean forward and place his forehead upon the floor. David said, "Who am I, O Lord GOD? and what is my house, that thou hast brought me hitherto? . . . thou hast spoken also of thy servant's house for a great while to come" (2 Sam. 7:18–19). David knew he was unworthy of such honor, and his words expressed humility when he said, "For thy word's sake, and according to thine own heart, hast thou done all these great things, to make thy servant know them" (verse 21). When David sat in the presence of God, he would have appreciated the words of Frederick C. Maker:

> Drop thy still dews of quietness,
> Till all our strivings cease;
> Take from our lives the strain and stress,
> And let our ordered lives confess
> The beauty of thy peace.

It is wise to take burdens to the Lord, and leave them there.

"Behold, I go forward, but he is not there; and backward,
but I cannot perceive him: On the left hand, where he doth work,
but I cannot behold him: he hideth himself on the right hand,
that I cannot see him: But he knoweth the way that I take;
when he hath tried me, I shall come forth as gold" (Job 23:8–10).

This statement made by Job was not exactly a promise; it was an affirmation of his faith. His world had been shattered. Friends insisted God had forsaken him, his family was dead, and his possessions were gone. The future remained bleak, yet in the darkness a light shone. He believed God and exclaimed, "When he hath tried me, I shall come forth as gold." Job was not a trained theologian. He was intensely human; every part of his life suffered except his faith. It is believed that Job was the first book of the Bible. If this view is correct, Job had no Scriptures to read and no prophets to whom he could go for advice. Job was one of the first saints to walk the earth. No sanctuary had been erected, and any knowledge gleaned from historical records was limited. Yet he communed with the Lord; his faith was mature, and although he failed to understand the reasons for the distressing circumstances, he believed God would help him to overcome.

The Ceaseless Annoyance . . . *Frustrating*

The account of the catastrophes that devastated the life and property of Job chills the human spirit. Within a short space of time he went from success to failure, prosperity to poverty, and supreme happiness to misery. Yet those terrible events could not compare with the frustration that haunted his soul. It appeared that God had deliberately hidden Himself, that He was indifferent to His servant's predicament. As the initial text indicated, Job said, "Behold, I go forward, but he is not there; and backward, but I cannot perceive him: On the left hand, where he doth work, but I cannot behold him; he hideth himself on the right hand, that I cannot see him." The distressed man looked in all directions hoping to find evidence of the Lord's compassion, but unfortunately, he searched in vain. He said, "I looked where he doth work," and that probably meant he remembered earlier places or circumstances when he had enjoyed fellowship with the Lord. Something had changed! God was no longer in the old haunts. He could not be dead, but was He offended? Other people have endured similar crises. Any man can praise God in times of supreme happiness, but only saints glorify Him when problems appear to be insurmountable.

The Courageous Acceptance . . . *Faithfulness*

Job never blamed God, but one of his statements indicated the limitation of his knowledge. He said, "Why died I not from the womb? . . . For now should I have lain still and been quiet . . . There the wicked cease from troubling, and there the weary be at rest" (see Job 3:11–17). His outlook was dismal. Death was the termination of existence. Therefore, it would be better to be dead than to remain alive suffering. Later in his experience that idea was challenged when he asked a very important question, "If a man die, shall he live again?" The value of the man's faith must be measured against the times in which he lived. He did not have the accumulated blessings of the Christian faith. He lived in a period when understanding of the Lord was limited. That enhanced the value of his testimony, "When he hath tried me, I shall come forth as gold." The patriarch did not understand the reason for his prolonged suffering, but his faith in the goodness of God remained unshaken. He believed that the Lord knew what was happening and seemed to be saying, "As long as God knows what He is doing, why should I worry? Eventually, I shall come forth as gold."

The Complete Assurance . . . *Fabulous*

Even in his lifetime Job knew the method used to refine gold. He looked upon his experiences as fire controlled by God who desired to see His reflection in the character of the tested saint. The patriarch apparently was willing to accept the process so the Refiner could gain His objective. That he ultimately came forth as predicted is proof of his spirituality. Even his loyalty toward friends remained undamaged. "And the LORD turned the captivity of Job, when he prayed for his friends; also the LORD gave Job twice as much as he had before" (Job 42:10). The saint did not realize he was the object of a direct attack from the powers of evil. He endured, and God was proud of him. His testimony should encourage all Christians who feel the Lord is slow answering prayers. A light shining in darkness is far more effective than one shining in the daylight!

*"Then came the word of the LORD to Isaiah, saying, Go, and
say to Hezekiah, Thus saith the LORD, the God of David thy father,
I have heard thy prayer, I have seen thy tears: behold, I will
add unto thy days fifteen years" (Isa. 38:4–5).*

The palace in Jerusalem was hushed; the musical instruments were silent. Hezekiah, the king, was gravely ill. Describing the scene Josephus wrote, "The physicians despaired of him, and expected no good issue of his sickness, as neither did his friends. And beside the distemper itself, there was a very melancholy circumstance that disordered the king, which was the consideration that he was childless, and was going to die, and leave his house and government without a successor of his own body" (*Antiquities of the Jews*, Book 10, chap. 2). Everyone believed Isaiah had made matters worse when he said to the king, "Set thine house in order: for thou shalt die, and not live" (Isa. 38:1). Afterward, the prophet returned to make the greatest promise Hezekiah ever heard. He claimed God had instructed him to say, "I have heard thy prayer, I have seen thy tears: behold, I will add unto thy days fifteen years."

A Dangerous Malady . . . *"Sick unto Death"*

Hezekiah was one of the best of Israel's kings, and although occasionally unwise, he endeavored to please God. The sickness which threatened his life was evidently some kind of boil or carbuncle. It is interesting to note that Isaiah advised that a poultice of figs be applied to the inflamed area. That ancient remedy is still widely used to make boils come to a head. "Recently, archeologists dug up a Babylonian tablet which stated that if a physician cut into a boil, and the patient died, the physician had both his hands cut off. If the patient happened to be a slave, the physician's hands were spared, but he had to buy another slave for the owner of the patient. So the doctor had to be extremely careful when he lanced an abscess or a boil" (*Zondervan Pictorial Encyclopedia of the Bible*, vol. 2, page 134). Isaiah was not a doctor, but he was an intimate friend of "the Great Physician" from whom he received instructions.

A Disturbing Message . . . *"Thou Shalt Surely Die"*

The promise of an extended life was unconditional. However, it was not given until Hezekiah wept bitter tears and uttered his prayer before the throne of God. When people are complacent and indifferent, it becomes necessary for the Lord to bring them to their senses.

God's ability is limitless, but sometimes, to get the best from His children, He works "in a mysterious way His wonders to perform." It seemed strange that Hezekiah should give to the Babylonians an escorted tour through the temple (see Isa. 39:1–2). His indiscretion led to the fall of his kingdom and the subjugation of his people. He was wiser on what might have been his deathbed than when he welcomed pagan emissaries.

A Distraught Monarch . . . "And Hezekiah Wept Sore"

At this time Hezekiah had no children, and it appeared he was more concerned with fathering a successor than regaining his health. To understand this, it is necessary to remember that among eastern potentates, to die without producing an heir to the throne was considered a disgrace. Barren women were thought to be cursed by the Lord. Kings who did not produce a son were also believed to be rejected by God. Even today, eastern kings never hesitate to divorce wives who fail to produce a male child. To Hezekiah the threat of death was terrible, but the thought of dying childless was worse. He forgot that the kingdom of Israel was far more important to God than to any other person.

A Definite Miracle . . . "I Will Add to Thy Days Fifteen Years"

The story of how God spoke to the prophet makes exciting reading. It is not difficult to visualize Isaiah's return to the distracted king. The calm dignity of God's servant contrasted with the pathetic appearance of the man who believed he was about to die. The physical recovery of Hezekiah was not a miracle; it was the result of the application of a poultice of figs which broke the abscess or boil. The extension of Hezekiah's life was a reminder that all life was controlled by the Almighty. When Daniel was threatened in Babylon, he solemnly said to king Belshazzar, "the God in whose hand thy breath is . . . hast thou not glorified" (Dan. 5:23).

The recovery of Hezekiah provided a glorious example of a truth enunciated by David. "For the LORD God is a sun and shield: the LORD will give grace and glory: no good thing will he withhold from them that walk uprightly" (Ps. 84:11).

"The voice of him that crieth in the wilderness, Prepare ye the way of the Lord, make straight in the desert a highway for our God. Every valley shall be exalted, and every mountain and hill shall be made low: and the crooked shall be made straight, and the rough places plain: And the glory of the Lord shall be revealed, and all flesh shall see it together: for the mouth of the Lord hath spoken it" (Isa. 40:3–5).

Isaiah wrote a Bible within a Bible! His first section (chapters 1–39) resembles the Old Testament; the second part (chapters 40–66) suggests the New Testament at the heart of which is chapter 53, a clear account of the death of Christ (see the author's book, *Bible Pinnacles*, pages 75–76). Isaiah's fortieth chapter is therefore the commencement of his "New Testament," and it begins with the ministry of John the Baptist—"a voice crying in the wilderness." There are three interpretations of this Scripture, each with its promise of approaching royalty.

The Promise of a Great Deliverance

The statement "Prepare ye the way of the Lord, make straight in the desert a highway for our God," was a reference to the custom of sending workmen ahead of a ruler to do whatever was necessary to facilitate the king's progress. It was often necessary to repair roads and move hills of sand so that the visiting monarch could make a triumphant entry into a city. Using that illustration, Isaiah proclaimed God would visit the captives in Babylon and servitude would end. He urged the Hebrews to repair the highways of life that the Lord's progress would not be hindered. Jeremiah supplied additional details of that great event. He wrote, "For thus saith the Lord, that after seventy years be accomplished at Babylon I will visit you, and perform my good word toward you, in causing you to return to this place. For I know the thoughts that I think toward you, saith the Lord, thoughts of peace and not of evil, to give you an expected end" (Jer. 29:10–11). These Scriptures with their repeated promises indicated (a) God's grace was greater than Israel's sin, (b) God saw the end from the beginning and knew what He was doing, and (c) no difficulty was too great for the Lord to overcome. These facts, when accepted in faith, turn darkness into light, despair into liberation, and disappointment into laughter.

The Promise of a Gracious Deliverer

Many years later John the Baptist used Isaiah's statement to inform listeners he was "the voice crying in the wilderness." He knew the King was approaching and urged everyone to prepare for His arrival (see Luke 3:3–6). The people were asked to remove obstacles from their highway of life. This was a vital part of John's message of repentance. Probably John was mindful of the astonishing effect of Christ's ministry. Valleys of depression would disappear as sufferers found new meaning in life. Mountains of difficulties would be removed, crooked lives made straight, and the roughest places in life made smooth. John quoted the text, "And all flesh shall see the salvation of God." People residing in Palestine were privileged to witness the healing power of Christ, but that hardly exhausted the meaning of the text, "*all flesh* shall see the salvation of God." It therefore becomes necessary to consider a third interpretation.

The Promise of a Glorious Domain

The text can never be completely fulfilled until the Lord returns to earth to establish His kingdom. Then the valleys will be exalted, and the high places will be made low when an earthquake divides the Mount of Olives. "And his feet shall stand in that day upon the mount of Olives . . . and the mount of Olives shall cleave in the midst thereof toward the east and toward the west, and there shall be a very great valley; and half of the mountain shall remove toward the north, and half of it toward the south" (Zech. 14:4). The reign of Christ will provide unprecedented opportunities for witnessing the power of God, for "the wolf also shall dwell with the lamb, and the leopard shall lie down with the kid . . . and a little child shall lead them" (Isa. 11:6).

This remarkable text touches every aspect of life; it embraces the past, present, and future. People who suffer in valleys of depression and others confronted by insurmountable obstacles find encouragement in the promises of Isaiah. Men and women who know the transforming power of Christ appreciate His ability to straighten crooked lives and smooth the rough places of life. Isaiah evidently believed it was wiser to consider the promises of God than to gaze dejectedly at the imprisoning walls of Babylon.

111

"Behold, the Lord GOD . . . He shall feed his flock like a shepherd: he shall gather the lambs with his arm, and carry them in his bosom, and shall gently lead those that are with young" (Isaiah 40:10–11).

The ancient prophets often referred to the Lord as "the Shepherd, a description that was easily understood by the Hebrews who had always raised sheep (see Gen. 46:31–47:3). Joseph was aware that shepherds were disliked by the Egyptians and was careful to avoid the displeasure of Pharaoh. When David contemplated accepting the challenge of Goliath, he informed Saul of exploits performed during his stay with the sheep on the hills of Bethlehem (see 1 Sam. 17:34–35). Centuries later, when the Savior addressed His followers, He said, "I am the good shepherd: the good shepherd giveth his life for the sheep" (see John 10:11). Isaiah's statement supplied three wonderful word pictures.

The Shepherd Leading . . . *A Great Provision*

"He shall feed his flock like a shepherd." Throughout the Middle East shepherds live with their sheep; they are never separated. The flock follows the leader and each day is led to places where pasture is available. He knows them individually, and they respond to his voice. Isaiah's conception of the loving kindness of the Lord was unsurpassed. Life could resemble a wilderness where sometimes sustenance was hard to find. It was the shepherd's duty to seek green pasture and still waters. The animals were never required to find grass, but they were expected to follow their guide. The Lord knew the terrain, and was an expert at finding pasture for His people.

The Shepherd Lifting . . . *A Gracious Protection*

"He shall carry the lambs with his arm." When newborn lambs could not travel as quickly as the rest of the flock, the shepherd lifted and cradled them in his arms. If they became exhausted with travel, he held them close to his heart. This supplied urgently needed protection. Every person who heard Isaiah's message could instantly visualized the scene. The inference that the Creator of the universe could be as tender as a boy who loved the lambs and led the flock was something difficult to comprehend. The Lord was not exclusively the stern and terrifying God whose presence made Mount Sinai tremble. Neither was He the devouring fire which threatened the existence of rebellious sinners. He was a God filled with compassion, a Heavenly Father who cared for His people. Perfect love for Him banished fear. The folk who trusted Him were never hungry!

The Shepherd Loving . . . *A Glorious Perception*

"And shall gently lead those that are with young." Sheep with special needs required added attention. Ewes giving suck to their offspring can become easy prey for predators. Wise shepherds gave instant attention to the mother sheep who in helping their young increased their own danger. During the lambing season in Western Australia, I often accompanied my host at midnight when the foxes tried to kill defenseless ewes. I did not realize until then the constant danger of sheep when they gave birth. That the Lord Jesus Christ should identify Himself as the Good Shepherd suggested that all the tendencies of a faithful shepherd would be evident in His care for men and women. His elderly sheep would neither be forsaken nor abandoned.

This text resembles the meat in a sandwich; it is between two expressions of the amazing power of the Lord. Isaiah said in verse 10, "Behold, the Lord GOD will come with strong hand, and his arm shall rule for him . . ." Then in verse 12, the prophet asked a very important question, "Who hath measured the waters in the hollow of his hand, and meted out heaven with the span, and comprehended the dust of the earth in a measure, and weighed the mountains in scales, and the hills in a balance?" The emphasis was upon the strong arm of the Almighty. God held the oceans in the palm of His hand; His reach encompassed the heavens, and with ease He lifted mountains and weighed them as in a scales. Even the greatest things in creation were as toys in the Lord's hand. Between these two statements Isaiah mentioned the ministry of the divine Shepherd. The hand that held mountains would hold and protect the lambs. That which held the seas controlled every wave of circumstance which threatened the welfare of God's sheep. George C. Stebbins wrote:

> O soul tossed on the billows
> Afar from a friendly land,
> Look up to Him who holds thee
> "In the hollow of His hand."

113

"But now thus saith the LORD. . . I have redeemed thee, I have called thee by thy name; thou art mine. When thou passest through the waters, I will be with thee; and through the rivers, they shall not overflow thee: when thou walkest through the fire, thou shalt not be burned; neither shall the flame kindle upon thee" (Isa. 43:1–2).

If baseball terminology were used to describe this text, then it touched all bases! It was one of the most majestic utterances ever made by the prophet. His collection of verses suggests a cluster of brilliant stars shining against the dark sky of human failure. It hardly needs an expositor. If Isaiah's writings were likened to a mountain range, this would be one of its highest peaks. Three glorious plateaus invite investigation.

Love Abounding . . . *How Undeserved*

"I have redeemed thee, I have called thee by thy name; thou art mine." This was truth in triplicate! It was all the more remarkable because earlier chapters of the book described a decadent nation. The Jews had forgotten and forsaken the Lord and ignored the appeal with which the prophet commenced his message. God said, "Come now, and let us reason together, saith the LORD: though your sins be as scarlet, they shall be as white as snow; though they be red like crimson, they shall be as wool" (Isa. 1:18). Unfortunately, the Lord's entreaty had been ignored; Israel continued to displease God. Their defiance of God's commandments and the continuing idolatry ruined their happiness. Their bondage in Babylon was thoroughly deserved. That the Lord could love such wayward people was hard to understand and impossible to explain. The poet expressed similar thoughts in his lines:

> How Thou canst think so well of us;
> And be the God Thou art:
> Is darkness to my intellect,
> But sunshine to my heart.

The Lord had redeemed Israel from Egypt and identified Himself with the nation which became His prized possession. The Jews enjoyed a special place among the nations. Christians can also claim the same privilege, for through the death of Christ redemption has been made possible. Believers may now address the Lord as "Heavenly Father." Their names are written in the Lamb's Book of Life. Redeemed sinners are the Lord's treasures. He bought us, He values us, and He protects us (see Mal. 3:17).

Love Assuring . . . *How Unlimited*

"When thou passeth through the waters, I will be with thee; and through the rivers, they shall not overflow thee." God never promised immunity from troubled waters. He said when rivers of difficulty were reached, sufficient strength would be provided to enable Israel to cross safely to the other side. God realized that ahead of His people were all kinds of problems which might threaten to sweep them away. Disaster would always be averted because He would hold back the waters—"they shall not overflow thee."

If the children of Israel never encountered "floods of difficulty," they would not have graduated from the school of experience. God often taught greater lessons in the river bed than He ever did on its banks! If the disciples of Jesus had not sailed through the storm on the Sea of Galilee, they would not have known the extent of Christ's ability to help them. That truth is demonstrated throughout the Scriptures. "When thou walkest through the fire, thou shalt not be burned; neither shall the flame kindle upon thee." The Hebrew boys who were thrown into Nebuchadnezzar's fire would have appreciated this wonderful text (see Dan. 3:22–25).

Love Abiding . . . *How Unsurpassed*

"Fear not for I am with thee: . . . Behold I will do a new thing . . . I give waters in the wilderness, and rivers in the desert, to give drink to my people, my chosen" (Isa. 43:5, 19,20). There was a definite sense in which these promises applied to the Hebrews, but since the promises of God are "Yea and Amen" in Christ, every Christian may discover continuing comfort in these announcements. The change from the tone of earlier statements was truly astonishing. Delitzsch, the German commentator, correctly said, "The sudden change from reproach to consolation was very significant. It gave them to understand that no meritorious work of their own would come in between what Israel was, and what it was to be . . . It was God's free grace which came to meet the need" (*Commentary on the Old Testament*, Vol. 7, page 2). The grace of God is an unfathomable ocean; without it, life would be impossible and the world a desert.

"Thus saith the LORD to his anointed, to Cyrus, whose right hand I have holden . . . I will give thee the treasures of darkness, and hidden riches of secret places, that thou mayest know that I, the LORD, which call thee by thy name, am the God of Israel" (Isa. 45:1–3).

This remarkable text mentions the only pagan king said to be the anointed of the Lord. The time of Israel's captivity in Babylon had seemed endless. The Lord, who saw the end from the beginning, predicted His anointed helper, the king of Persia, would overthrow the Babylon dynasty and liberate the enslaved Jews. Ultimately, the monarch heard how the God of heaven had predicted his victory, and this increased his determination to assist the unfortunate captives.

Isaiah's statement was exceptionally interesting. A heathen monarch had been chosen to aid the slaves. Did the Lord choose Cyrus because Hebrew deliverers were unavailable, or was the stranger given the assignment to indicate Gentiles were not beyond the reach of God's influence?

The "gates of brass, bars of iron, and the treasures of darkness" were unmistakable references to Babylon. The city had one hundred gates thought to have been made of wood, overlaid with brass. The gate posts were reinforced with iron. The accumulated wealth of the empire was stored in windowless vaults, and a second city named Sardes was the Fort Knox of Asia. It has been estimated that Cyrus confiscated treasure in excess of one hundred million dollars. Aware of God's help, he liberated the slaves, and thereby fulfilled the prediction made by Isaiah (see 2 Chron. 36:22–23). The promise regarding the treasures of darkness becomes even more instructive when applied to other areas of Scripture.

The Treasure of Indestructible Happiness (Acts 16:25)

It was very dark within the prison at Philippi; most of the prisoners were asleep. The events of the day had been frightening, and even the criminals were aware of the new men who had arrived bleeding and bruised. The inmates speculated as to the reason for their incarceration, and some of them might have assisted the suffering strangers. "And at midnight Paul and Silas prayed, and sang praises unto God: and the prisoners heard them." It was unbelievable, and even the official who rushed into the prison failed to comprehend what had happened. These men possessed joy which shone in darkness.

The Treasure of Inspiring Help (Matthew 14:22–33)

Money is one of the most valuable commodities in the world, but some of the most essential things in life cannot be purchased. The disciples had often endured storms on the Sea of Galilee but on this occasion were more afraid of the Man who walked on the water. "The ship was now in the midst of the sea, tossed with the waves: for the wind was contrary. And in the fourth watch of the night Jesus went unto them, walking on the sea. And when the disciples saw him walking on the sea, they were troubled." That terrifying experience in predawn darkness taught invaluable lessons: (a) Christ was greater than any storm; (b) No storm could endanger the life of a trusting soul as long as he obeyed his Lord; and (c) No storm could sink a ship if Christ were in it.

The Treasure of an Increasing Hope (Job 23:10)

The tragic yet triumphant story of Job's sufferings is probably one of the best known accounts in the Bible. The patriarch had won the respect of his fellow-citizens, and his place in ancient society is described in Job 29:5–25. Then, without warning, calamity fell upon that righteous man, and his serenity was ruined. Job could neither explain nor understand what had happened; it seemed God had forsaken him. Yet, throughout the darkness of his long ordeal, he never lost faith in the Lord, and the world now recognizes Job learned more in the darkness than he could have learned elsewhere.

The Treasure in an Indisputable Heartbreak (Luke 22:59–62)

Peter was ashamed and humiliated by memories. He had denied and dishonored the Lord and now believed he was beyond redemption. Even if the Lord pardoned his sin, Peter would never forgive himself! Paul described how the risen Christ appeared to Simon Peter before he was seen by any of the other apostles (see 1 Cor. 15:5). Perhaps the Savior sought Peter because the troubled disciple lacked the courage to rejoin his brethren. It is not known what the Lord said to His fallen follower, but evidently Christ's tenderness removed all bitterness from Peter's soul. Somewhere in the shadows that guilty man found a treasure of incalculable worth—it is called forgiveness.

117

*"When thou shalt make his soul an offering for sin, he shall see
his seed, he shall prolong his days, and the pleasure of the
Lord shall prosper in his hand. He shall see of the travail
of his soul, and shall be satisfied" (Isa. 53:10–11).*

The fifty-third chapter of Isaiah is among the most loved parts of
the Bible. Inspired by the Spirit of God, the prophet described in
detail all that would happen when the Messiah became the Redeemer of the world. The Scripture is all the more remarkable because
most of the contemporaries emphasized that when the Anointed
One arrived, He would subdue His enemies and establish the kingdom of God. Isaiah never contradicted his brethren; he merely insisted that to have a spiritual kingdom, it would be necessary to find
spiritual people over whom the Messiah could reign. The prophet
stated the kingdom would become a reality, but only after the Messiah had died to make reconciliation possible. Then he began to
elucidate the details of the crucifixion of Christ, and among his
promises or predictions was a statement which seemed to be ludi-
crous. Isaiah said a man would die giving birth to a baby.

The Messiah in Labor . . . *"The Travail of His Soul"*

The word "travail" was a word used for childbearing. A woman
about to give birth was described as "being in travail" (for example,
see Isa. 13:8; 21:3; 66:8; Jer. 31:8). Today that word has changed;
people speak of a woman being "in labor." Dr. Strong translated the
verse, "He shall see the fruit of His pain," and this corresponds with
the meaning of the text. To paraphrase Isaiah, "The Anointed One
will bring forth His baby; the first-fruits of a great family." The
exact time of this amazing event was clearly stated—"when thou
shalt make his soul an offering for sin." It was not to happen when
Christ healed the sick, gave sight to the blind, nor when He raised
the dead. Isaiah predicted it would take place when the Messiah
gave Himself "a ransom for many." That prediction was fulfilled
when the dying thief requested the Lord to help him get into the
kingdom of God. Christ would "see His seed." The magnitude of
that amazing miracle can only be understood in the light of Matthew's announcement that both thieves cursed the Lord (see Matt.
27:44). Perhaps Isaiah appeared to be foolish, but evidently he was
well-informed.

118

The Message of Love . . . *"Yet It Pleased the Lord to Bruise Him"*

I remember traveling on an overnight train from Edinburgh to London when a business man sat with me in the coach. We were both bored with the journey so I began a conversation. When I congratulated him on being a Jew, he was astounded, and asked, "How can you say that when you Gentiles believe the Jews crucified your Jesus?" I smiled and replied, "Sir, that is false. Neither Jews nor Gentiles crucified Jesus of Nazareth." He was puzzled, so I opened my Bible and asked if he believed the prophet Isaiah. When he replied, "Of course I do," I asked permission to read what the prophet said. "Yet it pleased the LORD to bruise him. *He hath put him to grief*" (Isa. 53:10). He listened when I explained it was not nails that kept Christ upon His cross, but the amazing love of God. Isaiah predicted the Messiah would "make his soul an offering for sin." Jesus "appeared to put away sin by the sacrifice of himself" (Heb. 9:26). When we separated in London, he supplied his business address and invited me to meet him again. I never had that opportunity, but what I said during the night was seed planted in fertile ground.

The Miracle of Liberation . . . *"He Shall Prolong His Days"*

Isaiah taught that the power of death would be vanquished; although the Messiah would die, He would rise again to attend to His Father's affairs —"the pleasure of the Lord shall prosper in his hand." The prophet said the Messiah would "justify many; for he shall bear their iniquities" (Isa. 53:11) The thief was the firstfruits of a tremendous harvest; many people would emulate his example, and the church would become a reality. It is understandable why orthodox Jews dislike this Scripture which remains one of the greatest pieces of literature ever written.

> So I'll cherish the old rugged cross,
> Till my trophies at last I lay down:
> I will cling to the old rugged cross,
> And exchange it some day for a crown.

*"And it shall come to pass, when seventy years are accomplished, that
I will punish the king of Babylon, and that nation, saith the LORD . . . And
I will bring upon that land all my words which I have pronounced
against it, even all that is written in this book, which Jeremiah hath
prophesied against all the nations" (Jer. 25:12–13).*

Seventy years represent a lifetime, but for Jewish captives in
Babylon that period seemed endless. The lament mentioned in Psalm
137 came from the depths of their souls. "By the rivers of Babylon,
there we sat down, yea, we wept, when we remembered Zion. We
hanged our harps upon the willows in the midst thereof. For there,
they that carried us away captive required of us a song; and they
that wasted us required of us mirth, saying, Sing us one of the songs
of Zion. How shall we sing the LORD's song in a strange land?" (Ps.
137:1–4). Memories of personal failure can be bitter!

Babylon was the greatest fortress in the ancient world. Its name
babili or *babilani*, meant "The gate of the gods." "Babylon was
encircled by a double system of defenses each comprising two walls.
The inner (Imger-Bel) was twenty-one feet thick and reinforced
with towers at sixty foot intervals. The outer (Nemit-Enlil) was
eleven feet in width and also had protruding watch-towers. About
six feet outside those ring walls, lay a brick lined key wall to
contain the waters fed from the Euphrates River, which formed a
flood defense" (*Zondervan Pictorial Encyclopedia of the Bible*, Vol.
1, pp. 441–442). That massive fortress was considered to be im-
pregnable.

A Sad Fate . . . The Silent Singers

The sorrow of the Jewish captives in Babylon was intense when
they said, "If I forget thee, O Jerusalem, let my right hand forget her
cunning. If I do not remember thee, let my tongue cleave to the roof
of my mouth" (Ps. 137:5–6). It was unnatural for such gifted people
to remain silent. The singers had lost their desire for music; their
hearts were broken, and their minds were filled with remorse. Successive generations had worshiped idols until finally the Lord permitted them to go to Babylon where idols stood on every street
corner. Each time the Jews saw pagans prostrating themselves before man-made deities, they were disgusted and asked, "How could

we have been so foolish to forget the God of our fathers?" Sometimes the Lord had to take drastic measures to open the eyes of people who had no desire to see! As the captives toiled in the unrelenting heat, they had sympathy for their ancestors who had toiled amid similar conditions in Egypt. Jeremiah promised that after seventy years God would send a deliverer, but when the older slaves remembered His words they wondered if he had made a mistake.

A Strange Fulfillment . . . *The Stirred Spirit*

The ancient historian wrote, "And them that had escaped from the sword carried he away to Babylon . . . to fulfil the word of the LORD by the mouth of Jeremiah . . . to fulfil three score and ten years. Now in the first year of Cyrus king of Persia, that the word of the LORD spoken by the mouth of Jeremiah might be accomplished, the LORD stirred up the spirit of Cyrus" (2 Chron. 36:20–22). God's timing was perfect. Cyrus could have attacked Babylon earlier or later, but everything was arranged according to the will of the Almighty, although Cyrus was unaware of what was taking place.

A Sublime Freedom . . . *The Splendid Start*

The conqueror of Babylon was a wise man; he thought of everything. Knowing some people would be unwilling to undertake the hazardous journey to Judah, he commanded those who preferred to remain to help those who accepted his challenge. Furthermore, all the treasures captured in the conquest of Israel were returned, and the money collected was considerable. Ezra reported, "And this is the number of them: thirty chargers of gold, a thousand chargers of silver, nine and twenty knives. Thirty basons of gold, silver basons of a second sort four hundred and ten, and other vessels a thousand. All the vessels of gold and silver were five thousand and four hundred" (Ezra 1:9–11). God knew how to supply the needs of His people, and it is a cause for thanksgiving that He still has that ability. David was wise when he said, "Commit thy way unto the LORD: trust also in him, and he shall bring it to pass" (Ps. 37:5).

"Verily I say unto you, Wheresoever this gospel shall be preached in the whole world, there shall also this, that this woman hath done, be told for a memorial of her" (Matt. 26:13).

Simon's house was very crowded; there was hardly room to move! The former leper had expressed to his friend, Martha, the desire to invite Jesus to supper. It was the least he could do to express the gratitude in his heart. Somewhere along the road of life he had met the Savior and had been transformed. Leprosy was expelled from his body, and a new experience had become possible. Jesus was about to visit Bethany, and Simon desperately wished to do something for his Benefactor. Yet his resources and skills were limited; he had no experience in entertaining visitors, and the prospect of welcoming twenty people frightened him. The Lord and His disciples would number thirteen; Martha's family increased that to sixteen, and a few neighbors would also be present. Simon smiled when he remembered Martha's expertise. She would help.

Supper had ended. Mary asked to be excused so she could make a quick visit to her home. After her return an altercation erupted in the sitting room. Apparently she had broken a box of very precious ointment and anointed the Savior's feet. Some of the disciples were complaining, "To what purpose was this waste? For this ointment might have been sold for much, and given to the poor" (Matt. 26:8–9). The voice of Jesus was heard clearly in the kitchen when He said, "Wheresoever this gospel shall be preached in the whole world, there shall also this, that this woman hath done, be told for a memorial of her." Suddenly the company was hushed; Jesus had made a remarkable statement.

A Promise Fulfilled . . . *How Reliable His Word*

Mary of Bethany was one of the few people who gave something to Jesus. The wise men brought gifts to the infant Christ, a lad gave his lunch, and someone offered a drink when Christ exclaimed, "I thirst." Perhaps the woman at Sychar's well responded when Jesus said, "Give me to drink" (see John 4:7), although the possibility exists that in the excitement which followed, she forgot His request and ran to the nearby city. Others asked Jesus to supper, but for devious reasons. The Pharisee invited the Lord but used the occasion to criticize his guest (see Luke 7:36–40). Only a few people spontaneously gave something to the Lord, but of that small number, Mary of Bethany received a special reward! Today, even in isolated jungle villages, natives know what happened in Simon's house. All women should be thrilled to remember these sisters of an earlier age. Mary, His mother, gave Jesus birth. Martha offered fellowship and food. A small company of dedicated women gave loving attention and dedicated service (see Matt. 27:55). The Lord never forgot those who ministered to His need.

A Problem Fermenting . . . *How Wise His Reply*

How Mary obtained her treasure is uncertain. Maybe she saved her money and bought it, or it might have been a present from her sister and brother or even a gift from a would-be suitor. She gave the best she had, but the disciples criticized her action. The suggested gift to the poor was possibly an excuse, hiding their avaricious desires. That the Lord interpreted the act as being an anointing for burial suggests three things: Her vision—she was aware of His approaching death; Her virtue—she desired to give her treasure while He was still alive; Her victory—personal desires were abandoned and she gave whole-heartedly. The Savior's response silenced the criticism that might have ruined the fellowship in that home. Her achievement was filled with merit. No person should offer to Christ anything less than the best.

A Person Favored . . . *How Gentle His Attitude*

The fragrance of that perfume was very noticeable; it filled the room, the small town, and, ultimately, it crossed oceans and filled continents. An ordinary woman who never preached, sang, nor took a prominent part in anything special gained international fame. Her deed was mentioned in the Word of God and sent on a worldwide mission. Yet it must not be forgotten the same fame was shared by a widow who placed two mites in the collection box at the temple. She probably did this unobstrusively, for she was embarrassed by the insignificance of her offering. Christ saw her action. Nothing can be hidden from Him. Fame is often a fleeting thing. People who gain applause from onlookers are often forgotten within a few months. To gain and maintain international fame is something rarely accomplished. Mary of Bethany discovered that secret, and so may we if nothing we possess is too valuable to lay at the Savior's feet.

*"Verily I say unto you, This generation shall not pass away,
till all be fulfilled. heaven and earth shall pass away: but
my words shall not pass away" (Luke 21:32–33).*

Among the many statements made by Christ, the promise concerning the enduring qualities of His Gospel was one of the greatest. That a Carpenter who lived among tools, wagons, and other equipment needing repair should express such amazing confidence staggers the imagination. Perhaps when He was a boy, Jesus attended the school of a rabbi, but He never studied in a college nor attended classes in a university. Yet He became the most sensational teacher of all time. Even by modern standards professors who know nothing of the Savior are not qualified to instruct students. The Carpenter from Nazareth is unavoidable! The verbal attacks of infidels supply evidence that they have been confronted by the Man of Galilee. It was to be expected that He who created the universe should be interested in the lilies of the field and concerned when a wounded sparrow fell to the ground. It is now recognized that the One who held children in His arms could have explained problems that baffle earth's greatest scientists. Although enemies scoffed at His statements and ridiculed His words, Christ said His message would never be forgotten. After nearly two thousand years three facts endorse His claim.

Its Miraculous Preservation

The survival of a book depends upon its message, charm and accuracy. The United States of America produces over 80,000 new volumes every year, but these are only a small part of the eight billion books printed annually throughout the world. Many are only printed once. Unsatisfactory sales result in their early disappearance from bookstores. Only a very limited number are reprinted after twenty years, and the greatest books are often forgotten after one generation. Even the most ardent students have difficulty locating a book printed centuries ago. If a desired copy is found in an ancient library, it is beyond the purchasing power of millionaires. It is a challenging fact, therefore, that the Bible, one of the oldest books in existence, may be purchased for a nominal sum at any bookstore.

History records that throughout the centuries copies of the Scripture were confiscated by authorities and burned in an attempt to destroy Christianity. Those who preached its message were executed, but the death of the martyrs became the seed of the church. The Bible proved itself to be indestructible! When its pages were destroyed by fire, the message survived in the memories of Christians and was reproduced by those who cherished the Word of God. This cannot be claimed for any other book.

Its Matchless Predictions

When Jesus taught throughout Galilee, some of His listeners questioned His authority for making what they considered to be outrageous statements! The religious leaders of the time accused the Lord of blasphemy. Nevertheless, Jesus continued to speak of the future as if He were describing what had already happened. He spoke of His death and resurrection, the destruction of the temple, the descent of the Holy Spirit, and the exploits of men who were to support His cause. He predicted His return to earth and said His kingdom, which at one time appeared insignificant, would eventually offer shelter to all nationalities. After two thousand years His accuracy has become evident to everybody. There cannot be many places on earth where His name remains unknown. Roman emperors tried to destroy the church; preachers of the Gospel were beaten, imprisoned, and burned to death. Yet, where Christians died the church continued to survive. This could not have been a coincidence!

Its Marvelous Power

The greatest evidence to prove the inspiration of the Bible is its ability to transform lives; one testimony is worth a ton of theology. Centuries ago a beggar confronted by the arguments of learned men replied, "One thing I know, that, whereas I was blind, now I see" (John 9:25). The story has been told of an infidel who was in the process of taking tons of communist literature to South Africa. Sailing on the same ship was a Salvation Army missionary. Eventually, the two met and began to discuss the merits of Christianity. The man began to gloat over the inability of the young lady to offset his reasoning. Suddenly, the Christian began to weep, saying, "I cannot destroy your arguments, but you cannot destroy my love for the Savior." The tears terminated the discussion, but before the ship arrived in Cape Town, the man had thrown overboard all his literature. It is difficult to argue against changes! Christ promised His message would be indestructible!

"But ye shall receive power, after that the Holy Ghost is come upon you: and ye shall be witnesses unto me both in Jerusalem, and in all Judaea, and in Samaria, and unto the uttermost part of the earth" (Acts 1:8).

This promise was one of the Savior's most sensational utterances. He was about to leave His disciples with a very formidable task. When David confronted Goliath, he knew he only had one antagonist. When the giant fell, the Philistines fled. The disciples of Jesus did not have that consolation. The opposition of the Jewish leaders would never cease, and the animosity of the Romans would continue as long as the empire existed. The fishermen from Galilee had limited intellectual ability; they were ordinary people such as those found on any beach around the Sea of Galilee. They were to represent their Master on a very special mission.

Nevertheless, they were overwhelmed with apprehension for circumstances had drastically changed. The Master's warning was disturbing, "They shall lay their hands on you, and persecute you, delivering you up to the synagogues, and into prisons, being brought before kings and rulers for my name's sake" (Luke 21:12). The prospect of martyrdom was not pleasant. The exponents of the new faith would be beaten and tortured until death. They were being asked to do the impossible—to survive a political crisis which apparently would never end. Yet Jesus promised a different kind of assistance; the Holy Spirit would become the Leader of the crusade to reach the world and would impart strength to the evangelists. The Lord's promise was exciting, but perhaps beyond their comprehension. "Ye shall receive power after that the Holy Ghost is come upon you." Certain facets of this stirring promise quickly became evident.

Power to Perceive . . . *Their Essential Message*

The Greek word *dunamin* occurs in 130 places within the New Testament. It is translated as: power (Acts 1:8); mighty works (Matt. 11:20); virtue (Luke 6:19); miracles (Acts 2:22); strength (2 Cor. 1:8); might (Col. 1:11); abundance (Rev. 18:3). Explaining the word, Dr. Thayer says, "It meant inherent power, strength and ability." It suggests incomparable might and ability to do the extraordinary; biblical writers used it to express something superlative. The Lord said, "I have yet many things to say unto you, but ye cannot bear them now. Howbeit when he, the Spirit of truth, is come, he will guide you into all truth" (John 16:12–13). The instruction to be given by the Holy Spirit would enable listeners to understand the Scriptures regarding the Messiah. He would be heaven's professor sent to help students.

Power to Preach . . . *Their Exciting Ministry*

The two outstanding preachers within the early church were Simon Peter and Stephen. Unfortunately, although Peter was eloquent, his subject matter was limited and his attitude not above reproach. Stephen was a more charming orator and well-versed in the Scriptures. Unfortunately, he was destined to become the first martyr of the church, and would play no part in world evangelism. The disciples had experience in itinerant preaching, but there is no record they had ever won a convert. Doubtless Peter and the others did their best to represent Christ, but that was insufficient to meet the challenge of the future. They would stand before educated listeners and ruthless monarchs. They needed to learn how to handle such threatening situations. Peter's efforts on the Day of Pentecost indicated the Holy Spirit had taken control of His servant. The Savior said, "But ye shall receive power, *after* that the Holy Ghost is come upon you." Educational attainments are of superlative worth; oratorical ability may be developed, but Simon Peter had no time to develop anything! When the Holy Spirit took possession of him, the immature preacher became *dunamis*—dynamite!

Power to Prevail . . . *Their Extensive Mission*

What Peter and his colleagues did on the Day of Pentecost was remarkable, but only Paul demonstrated the full extent of the promise made by Jesus. The disciples were content to linger in Jerusalem, and their commission was almost forgotten. When Saul of Tarsus became a Christian, he commenced an extensive crusade to reach the known world. It was a task that the disciples should have already commenced. Perhaps inspired by Paul's example, some of the apostles traveled to other nations, but Paul alone was the spearhead of Christian enterprise. His untiring efforts laid the groundwork for world evangelism (see also the author's commentary *The Amazing Acts*, pp. 24-25).

*"I have appeared unto thee for this purpose, to make thee a
minister and a witness . . . delivering thee from the people,
and from the Gentiles, unto whom now I send thee . . . And
Paul dwelt two whole years in his own hired house, and received
all that came in unto him" (Acts 26:16–17; 28:30).*

The city of Caesarea was filled with excited people. King Agrippa and his wife, Bernice, were making an official visit. In honor of
the occasion, Festus had made arrangements to make the event
memorable. Everything proceeded according to plan until Festus
informed Agrippa of the strange prisoner left behind by his prede-
cessor, Felix. The king's curiosity was aroused, and Agrippa expressed a desire to hear the incarcerated preacher. An audience was
hurriedly arranged, and ultimately Paul entered with chains hanging
from his wrists and ankles. The apostle looked at the assembled
audience, but when he realized the importance of the occasion, his
eyes shone.

He said, "Yes, O King, Jesus, who rose from the grave, said to
me: I have appeared unto thee for this purpose . . . Delivering thee
from the people, and from the Gentiles, unto whom now I send
thee: To open their eyes, and to turn them from darkness to light.'"
Paul's eyes were misty as he reminisced! He seemed to emphasize
the words, "the Gentiles unto whom now I send thee." Beyond the
mountains and oceans were people who had never heard about
Jesus. They were to become his parishioners. He had traveled ex-
tensively on his missionary journeys but was convinced his task had
not been completed. He was old, and his strength diminished. Travel was a burden. How could he complete his mission?

The Illustrious Counselor . . . *Attracting*

It was said that all roads led to Rome. The Caesars had established a far-reaching empire; trade, news, and soldiers moved quickly
in all directions. Paul knew this, but how he would be taken to the
city was planned by God. At no expense to Paul, he was taken to
the imperial city and after an appearance before the emperor was
granted freedom. He rented a house somewhere within the city and
established a home. It became evident that when the apostle was
unable to visit foreign lands, God arranged that people of all nations
would come to Rome.

The International Congregation . . . *Absorbing*

There was much to be seen within the city of Caesar, but when Paul lived in his "own hired house," his home was more attractive than temples. Men spoke of the strange man whose residence had become the most interesting place in the city. It was common knowledge that many people desired to hear the doctrines that disturbed the philosophers. "There came many to him into his lodging; to whom he expounded and testified the kingdom of God, persuading them concerning Jesus, both out of the law of Moses, and out of the prophets, from morning till evening" (Acts 28:23). The statement "none forbidding him" was used frequently by medical writers to denote freedom, unhindered action in a variety of things such as respiration, perspiration, the pulse, and the muscles (Hobart). Every day Roman citizens and foreign visitors listened to Paul, and some of these people became missionaries. For example, Caracticus, a Celtic chief captured by the Romans, earned his freedom during his captivity in Rome. Having heard the Gospel (perhaps from Paul), he returned to evangelize his own people. It is believed he was the first Christian missionary to preach in Britain. The slave Onesimus also was led to Christ by Paul, and the letter to Philemon indicated the reality of the fugitive's conversion.

The Inspired Converts . . . *Acknowledging*

It would be interesting to know who paid the rent for Paul's home. As a prisoner he would have little, if any, financial resources. Perhaps the local church supported him. From time to time the churches established through the apostle's ministry sent love offerings to supply his need (see Phil. 4:16). During his stay in Rome, Paul wrote several epistles. How he found time to write during his busy schedule remains a mystery, but his untiring efforts enriched the world. The apostle's imprisonment, considered by many to have been regrettable, was overruled by God to accomplish the impossible. Evidently, the Lord knew what He was doing! Paul never wasted time, and neither should we, if we desire to receive a crown (see 2 Tim. 4:6–8).

"Howbeit we must be cast upon a certain island" (Acts 27:26).

Stars are best seen on dark nights, and God's promises are appreciated most when circumstances suggest their fulfillment to be impossible. Blessed is the person who can stand on a sinking ship and exultantly cry, "I believe God!" For two terrifying weeks Paul's ship had drifted out of control. The captain and his men were completely helpless, and all hope of reaching land had been lost. The sailors were brave, but under those conditions even the strongest men trembled. They had been lost in the darkness, and the ceaseless noise of huge waves battering the ship intensified their fear. The vessel was about to splinter and break in pieces, and the sea would be their grave. Luke, in describing that scene, said, "And when neither sun nor stars in many days appeared, and no small tempest lay on us, all hope that we should be saved was then taken away" (Acts 27:20).

The Man Who Listened . . . *Carefully*

"For there stood by me this night the angel of God, whose I am, and whom I serve, Saying, Fear not Paul: thou must be brought before Caesar and, lo, God hath given thee all them that sail with thee" (vv. 23–24). The other people aboard the stricken vessel heard only the noise of the tempest. Paul resembled Elijah of whom it is written, "And, behold, the LORD passed by, and a great and strong wind rent the mountains . . . and after the wind an earthquake . . . And after the earthquake a fire . . . and after the fire a still small voice. And it was so, when Elijah heard it, he wrapped his face in his mantle" (1 Kings 19:11–13). Paul and Elijah were expert listeners, and so are all who spend time in God's presence. It is better to listen than to complain!

The Man Who Learned . . . *Continually*

When God speaks, He says something important; when His children listen, they learn! Paul was assured that his companions would be saved from drowning, but he was also given a magnificent example of the unerring wisdom of God. He was informed that the vessel would be cast upon a certain island.

"The Mediterranean is an inland sea lying between the continents of Europe, Asia, and Africa . . . in a nearly east and west direction, it is about 2400 miles in length . . . . Its width varies from

1000 miles to less than 100 miles . . . . The area of the Mediterranean is estimated at 965,000 square miles . . . . The area of Malta is 95 square miles" (*Funk and Wagnal Encyclopedia*, Vol. 16, pp. 4,790, 5,948). Without a chart and compass and in the middle of a tempest, it would be impossible to find such a small island. It would be easier to find a needle in the proverbial haystack!

The Man Who Laughed . . . *Confidently*

If another person had spoken those words, Paul would have been justified in rejecting the message. Yet, he believed God and with confidence relayed the message to his companions. He said, "Wherefore, sirs, be of good cheer: for I believe God, that it shall be even as it was told me" (Acts 27:25). Possibly he smiled as he gave his message and overcame unbelief with laughter. He had heard the promise of God and never questioned its accuracy. If God held the universe in His hand, He would not have trouble steering a ship in a storm.

The Man Who Led . . . *Courageously*

James said, "Faith without works is dead" (James 2:20). Paul believed the same truth for "While the day was coming on, Paul besought them all to take meat, saying . . . this is for your health: for there shall not an hair fall from the head of any of you. And when he had thus spoken, he took bread, and gave thanks to God in the presence of them all" (Acts 27:33–35). It was too dark and difficult for the sailors to see God, but they saw and heard Paul and that was all they needed.

The Man Who Loved . . . *Completely*

The apostle not only loved his Lord, he loved everybody! His parish was the world, and wherever he journeyed, he became an inspiration to listeners. His example thrilled the churches; he was the greatest of all missionaries. People seldom complained when he asked them to sacrifice, for they knew he had given everything for Christ and world evangelism. Probably he was the greatest of all theologians, for he wrote most of the New Testament. Yet greater than his knowledge and more far reaching than his travels was the example set before his friends. Writing to the Christians in Corinth, he said, "And though I have all faith, so that I could remove mountains, and have not charity, I am nothing" (1 Cor. 13:2).

GOD, WHO MADE THE GREATEST
PROMISE OF ALL TIME

"Eternal life, which God, that cannot lie,
promised before the world began" (Titus 1:2).

I knew a charming young lady, a student in an American university, who had an intellectual problem. Aware of the pain throughout the world, she could not understand how God, who saw the end from the beginning, could possibly have created man in the first instance. She believed the suffering could have been prevented if God had been more considerate! When I was a young student, I also had a similar difficulty.

Then one day I saw the adoration in a young mother's eyes as she adoringly looked at her chuckling baby. Throughout my ministry, I have watched tears of joy running down the faces of men and women as they endeavored to describe their happiness in knowing Christ. I listened to the song of a lark and saw a kitten becoming increasingly tangled as it played with a ball of yarn. I have been enthralled watching a boy playing with his puppy, and I asked would God have been fair to prevent such happiness because some people preferred to sin? Would the Almighty have been fair to Himself and us had He refused to create human beings? Even the angels might have said, "When He had a chance to do something good, He refused." Paul's letter to Titus introduced readers to a promise made before time began.

God Promised

The apostle mentioned something which took place before the commencement of the ages. There were no stars twinkling in the heavens, and life existed only in the eternal Trinity. Somewhere in the depths of ageless infinity, Omniscience convened a meeting. The agenda was intriguingly simple, yet overwhelmingly difficult—how to bring order out of chaos, to bring beauty out of nothing, to fill a limitless void with charm, and to enable human beings to enjoy sinless immortality. The results and implications of that meeting baffle the mind. The creation of angels and men were considered, and at some point during the proceedings, the omnipotent God made a promise. Far down the corridor of what was to be time, He saw a world filled with people and promised to offer them eternal life. That was the first promise ever made. It is almost impossible to decide to whom the commitment was made. Did God promise Himself? Did He make the promise to the Word, who was in the beginning with God? Did He make it to the unborn millions of people who were destined to be the recipients of a treasure only He could provide?

God Planned

At some point in that meeting, the possible failure of the project was considered. What if man should sin and become unfit to cooperate in the project? What then could be done to prevent eternal disaster and salvage what remained of the initial program? Was the Lord, the Everlasting Father, surprised when the Word calmly said, "If man fails, then I will assume the responsibility for his failure. Since the laws of righteousness will demand retribution, I will take his sin, pay his penalty, and restore his opportunity to obtain an eternal home in your presence." John referred to that occasion when he wrote of "the Lamb slain from the foundation of the world" (Rev. 13:8). It became evident to John that God foresaw human guilt and found a way by which to circumvent the problem. Perhaps it was at this juncture the Father said to the Son, "If you will do this, then in your name, I promise to give eternal life to whomsoever you sponsor?"

God Persevered

God knew His people would need a home in which to live, and He provided it. "And the Spirit of God moved upon the face of the waters. And God said, Let there be light, and there was light" (Gen. 1:2–3). From that thrilling beginning, the Lord's creative work continued until the earth became a place of entrancing beauty. "And God saw that it was good" (v. 25). Then with pride and joy, God said, "Let us make man in our image, after our likeness" (v. 26). Life was breathed into dust, and man became a living soul. Afterward, He made Eve. "She was lovely; she was indescribably charming; dignified as befitting a queen of creation, as refreshing as the morning dew. Her eyes were lit with curiosity and expectation as she scanned her surroundings. Her movements were graceful and effortless, and when she spoke, pleasure filled the Creator's heart. She was fascinatingly beautiful, she was good, and she was very desirable. 'And the Lord God brought her to man.'" (see the author's book, *Bible Pinnacles*, p. 1). The Gospel reveals how God fulfilled the first promise that was ever made.

"Jesus Christ the same yesterday, and to day, and for ever" (Heb. 13:8).

Age changes everything! The top came off the pyramid of Giza. The weather effects the carved faces on Mount Rushmore. Machines of all kinds need to be repaired and ultimately removed from service. The weather, sky, and ocean may change within hours, and the opinions of people within minutes. H. F. Lyte wrote, "Change and decay in all around I see; O Thou, Who changest not, abide with me." The Bible declares that Jesus Christ remains the same. He came to earth, lived, and died as a man, but when His body "put on immortality," He never changed again. Among the promises of God is the jewel of everlasting worth.

Everlasting Life . . . *A Purpose Performed*

"In hope of eternal life, which God, that cannot lie, promised before the world began" (Titus 1:2). "Verily, verily, I say unto you, He that heareth my word, and believeth on him that sent me, hath everlasting life" (John 5:24). Paul affirmed that God, even from eternity, promised eternal life to people who conformed to His will. The teaching of the Savior confirmed and endorsed that fact.

Everlasting Redemption . . . *A Price Paid*

"Neither by the blood of goats and calves, but by his own blood he entered in once into the holy place, having obtained eternal redemption for us" (Heb.9:12). The Savior obtained *eternal* redemption, and this implies His death covered every eventuality. It not only reached back into time, but also guaranteed the future needs of redeemed people will be supplied.

Everlasting Salvation . . . *A Plan Perfected*

"But Israel shall be saved in the LORD with an everlasting salvation: ye shall not be ashamed nor confounded world without end" (Isa. 45:17). This verse presents a magnificent progression of thought. What was purposed before time began was made possible through the death of Christ and given by Him to repentant sinners. The words were spoken primarily to Israel, but "all the promises of God in him are yea, and in him Amen, unto the glory of God by us" (2 Cor. 1:20).

Everlasting Fatherhood . . . *A Parent Protecting*

"For unto us a child is born, unto us a son is given: and the government shall be upon his shoulder: and his name shall be called Wonderful, Counseller, The mighty God, the everlasting Father, The Prince of Peace" (Isa. 9:6). "Philip saith unto him, Lord, shew us the Father, and it sufficeth us. Jesus saith unto him . . . he that hath seen me hath seen the Father" (John 14:8–9). Acceptance of Christ commences a unique relationship between the sinner and God. "But as many as received him, to them gave he power to become the sons of God, even to them that believe on his name" (John 1:12).

Everlasting Joy . . . *A Pleasure Persisting*

"And the ransomed of the LORD shall return, and come to Zion with songs and everlasting joy upon their heads: they shall obtain joy and gladness, and sorrow and sighing shall flee away" (Isa. 35:10). Doubtless this prediction concerned the return of the captives from Babylon, but that was only a foreshadowing of the happiness to be known by those who found redemption in Christ. People who surrender to the Savior rejoice in the goodness of the Lord. "And the disciples were filled with joy, and with the Holy Ghost" (Acts 13:52).

Everlasting Kindness . . . *A Pleasantness Prevailing*

"In a little wrath I hid my face from thee for a moment; but with everlasting kindness will I have mercy on thee, saith the LORD thy Redeemer" (Isa. 54:8). This revelation was vastly different from the the Lord whose frightening presence shook Mount Sinai. God's love for His people was beyond comprehension.

Everlasting Consolation . . . *A Peace Pervading*

"Now our Lord Jesus Christ himself . . . hath given us everlasting consolation and good hope through grace" (2 Thess. 2:16). The word translated consolation or encouragement is *parakleesin*. It was used by the Lord to describe the Holy Spirit. "For if I go not away, the Comforter (Paraclete) will not come unto you" (John 16:7). The continuing Presence of the divine Spirit guarantees continuous consolation and help for God's children.

Everlasting Arms . . . *A Power Providing*

"The eternal God is thy refuge, and underneath are the everlasting arms" (Deut. 33:27). This probably is the greatest of all the implied promises. It guarantees the arms and hands which hold the universe will have no difficulty protecting us! There can never be an emergency with which God cannot cope! "When I fear my faith will fail, He will hold me fast."

THE PROMISE OF A LIGHT AT
THE END OF THE TUNNEL

"Blessed is the man that endureth temptation: for when he is tried, he shall receive the crown of life, which the Lord hath promised to them that love him" (James 1:12).

The Epistle written by James expresses the practical side of the Christian faith. The apostle appreciated sound doctrine but insisted faith without works is dead (see James 2:17). He never mentioned the Incarnation, redemption through the blood of Christ, nor the Resurrection. Apparently the basic facts of the faith were not as important as dedicated conduct. Perhaps he was disillusioned with disappointing people who professed to be followers of the Lord. He was not as interested in the three thousand converts won at Pentecost as he was with the number remaining active for Christ five or ten years after their professed conversion. The apostle wrote of faithfulness and endurance and insisted "Pure religion and undefiled before God and the Father is this, To visit the fatherless and widows in their affliction, and to keep himself unspotted from the world" (James 1:27). Difficulties were a tunnel through which the faithful would travel. He believed there was always a light shining at the end of the road. There were crowns to be won, and Christians should not risk losing their rewards.

A Crown of Life . . . *The Blessing of Endurance* (James 1:12)

"The man that endureth temptation . . . he shall receive the crown of life." James believed eternal life was a gift offered to undeserving sinners, but he proceeded to emphasize other features of discipleship. Even Jesus had warned His followers, saying, "If any man will come after me, let him deny himself, and take up his cross, and follow me" (Matt. 16:24). The church was not a haven for cowards! Christians would be required to die for their Master. Some would be fed to lions, and others burned at the stake. If heaven were a desired destination, then pilgrims should rejoice as they approached the end of their journey. James suggested that Christians should act and talk and even dress like people whose home lay beyond this world; they should be holy. Such conduct might lead to sorrow and suffering, but those who remained faithful would receive "the crown of life." That was the light at the end of the tunnel.

A Crown of Righteousness . . . *The Reward of Expectancy* (2 Timothy 4:8)

Looking back Paul said, "I have fought a good fight, I have finished my course, I have kept the faith" (2 Tim. 4:7). Looking forward, he was able to say, "Henceforth there is laid up for me a crown of righteousness." The apostle who had walked through dark tunnels of adversity was approaching the end of his pilgrimage when Christ would give to him a crown of righteousness. Paul believed that all who looked for the appearance of the Savior would share in a similar experience.

A Crown of Rejoicing . . . *The Reward of Evangelism* (1 Thessalonians 2:19)

"For what is our . . . crown of rejoicing? Are not even ye in the presence of our Lord Jesus Christ at his coming?" John wrote, "I have no greater joy than to hear that my children walk in truth" (3 John 4). Paul's happiness was even more intense when he considered meeting converts at the feet of Jesus. Nothing could supersede the thrill of hearing "Thank you for introducing me to the Savior." To wear a crown is an ultimate! A prince may be elated, but to ascend the throne is a greater honor. Paul believed one of his most thrilling moments in heaven would be his meeting with those whom he had won for Christ.

A Crown of Incorruption . . . *The Reward of Elegance* (1 Corinthians 9:24–25)

The apostle wrote, "Know ye not that they which run in a race, run all, but one receiveth the prize. So run, that ye may obtain . . . Now they do it to obtain a corruptible crown: but we an incorruptible." Doubtless, he was considering athletes who worked hard for the dubious distinction of winning a diadem of parsley! Christians should strive even more to win eternal rewards. The elegance of this eternal recognition would be known throughout God's kingdom.

A Crown of Glory and Honor . . . *The Reward of Emmanuel* (Hebrews 2:7)

It was a wonderful moment, when after returning from His mission on earth, the Savior was crowned "with glory and honor." That occasion had been typified by the crowning of Israel's high priest. That was a symbolic act performed when the national intercessor was initiated into his important office. The Lord Jesus Christ fulfilled that type when He became the High Priest of His church. The magnificence of that event begs description, for the Lord was honored before the assembled hosts of heaven. Could it be possible —if only in a lesser sense—that God will also honor those saints in whose service He finds merit? One smile from the Lord will more than compensate for all the trials ever endured.

Promises Awaiting Fulfillment

THE PROMISE OF AN AMAZING LAND GRANT

"In the same day, the LORD made a covenant with Abram, saying, Unto thy seed have I given this land, from the river of Egypt unto the great river, the river Euphrates" (Gen. 15:18).

The promise of God's land grant to Abram has created considerable discussion among theologians. The patriarch, who had recently arrived in Canaan, was a stranger in a new land. Although he was wealthy by ancient standards, he possessed nothing except the flocks and herds which he brought from Haran. The description of his meeting with the Lord was mysterious and startling. "And it came to pass, that, when the sun went down, and it was dark, behold a smoking furnace, and a burning lamp that passed between those pieces" (Gen. 15:17). Did Abram sleep and dream, or was this a vision? Later, he described how he saw a smoking furnace and a lamp that moved in the darkness. As he contemplated the meaning of these things, God said, "Unto thy seed have I given this land, from the river of Egypt unto the great river, the river Euphrates."

The eastern boundary of this land grant was clearly defined. The seed of Abraham would inherit all the territory which reached to the river Euphrates. That was an enormous amount of land. The western boundary was not so definitive. The text mentioned "the river of Egypt" which according to some writers was the Nile, the lifeline of the country. The commentators Keil, Kurtyz, Hungstenburg, and Kalitsch agree with this interpretation. However, in Bible times the border of Egypt was the *Wady el Arish* which was named "the Brook of Egypt." This was at the southern extremity of the land into which Abram had come. The writers Knobel, Lange, and Clark believe this was the southwestern limit of Abram's inheritance.

It is significant that the seed of Abraham never possessed that land. Reference to the *Wady el Arish* was made when the land was divided among the occupying tribes of Israel (Num. 34:5; Josh. 15:4; Isa. 27:12). During the reigns of David and Solomon most, but not all, of that territory was occupied by the armies of Israel (1 Kings 4:21; 2 Chron. 9:26). When the debates and arguments are concluded, one fact remains: the seed of Abraham never acquired those territories. Therefore, the complete fulfillment of the ancient promise must take place in the future. Perhaps this will not be completely fulfilled until the millennial reign of Christ when the entire earth will belong to His kingdom.

Nevertheless, "if coming events cast their shadows before," the return of Israel to her homeland must be one of the greatest events in history. The Jews who had been scattered to all parts of the earth, who possessed no national home, and had endured unprecedented persecution, are now established in their ancient homeland. Continuing attacks by terrorists disturb the serenity of the land, and this can be seen on the west bank of the Jordan River. Arabs claim the land belongs to them, but Orthodox Jews assert the territory was given to the seed of Abraham long before any Arab existed, quoting the promise made by the Lord. Perhaps their claim is legitimate, for God stated, "But my covenant will I establish with Isaac, which Sarah shall bear unto thee at this set time in the next year" (Gen. 17:21). The Arab nations belong to the seed of Abraham, but they descended from Ishmael rather than Isaac.

God named ten nations which occupied the promised land; these were ultimately reduced to seven, probably because some had been destroyed or had united with other tribes. Today's maps indicate the Euphrates runs through Iraq to the Persian Gulf. Israel is being asked to relinquish territory now in her possession, but if the ancient promise made to Abraham is to be literally fulfilled, the Jewish people in some sensational way will acquire even more territory. How this will be accomplished may remain a mystery until it happens.

Modern Israel attracts more attention than any other country. Jerusalem was dominated by Gentile nations from the days of Nebuchadnezzar who lived in the sixth century before Christ. Today it is the capital city of the State of Israel. The eyes of the world are focused upon the Middle East to see if God intends to fulfill the promises made to Abraham.

*"For they shall suck of the abundance of the seas,
and of treasures hid in the sand" (Deut. 33:19).*

The tribes of Israel were apprehensive; their leader Moses was about to leave his people. Canaan was ahead, but everyone realized an indiscretion had deprived the patriarch of the privilege of entering the land of milk and honey. Moses seemed resigned to his loss, but his eyes were gleaming as he expressed a desire to bless the tribes. His words proved he was a true prophet. Unerringly, he explained the future, but of all the predictions his message concerning Zebulun was most intriguing. He described how the tribesmen would assemble for celebrations of praise and righteousness, and suggested their gratitude would be occasioned by the discovery of hidden treasure in the seas and sand.

It is exceedingly interesting to read the interpretations given by older commentators. Compared with modern writings, their comments appear to be "quaint." For example, Keil and Delitzsch state, "The thought expressed is, that the riches and treasures of both sea and land would flow to the tribes of Israel" *(Commentary on the Old Testament,* Vol. 1, "Deuteronomy," page 508). The prosperity to be known during the millennial reign of Christ would best be seen among the people over whom He reigned. Matthew Henry said, "Zebulon that goes abroad, shall suck of the abundance of the seas, which are [milk] to the merchants." Jamieson, Fausset and Brown say, "Both tribes (Zebulun and Issachar) should traffic with the Phoenicians in gold and silver, pearl and coral, especially in murex, the shell fish that yielded the famous Tyrian dye; and in glass, which was manufactured from the sand of the river Belus in their immediate neighborhood." Adam Clark wrote, "They shall be very prosperous in coastal voyages, for this tribe's situation was favorable for traffic, having many seaports. . . . As Zebulun would be prosperous in shipping and trade, Issachar would be in agriculture and pasturage."

It is difficult to read the comments of these great men without remembering they lived in an earlier century. Evidently they considered the term "nurse" to be figurative, which explains Matthew Henry's reference to the seas contributing to the wealth of merchants. Today it is believed sucking treasure from sea and sand refers to oil. When Moses made his statements to the tribes of

Israel, he knew that in the end times God's people would become wealthy because of the discovery of oil fields.

The territory promised to Abraham's seed far exceeds what today is known as Israel (see Abraham's "Original Land Grant" in this book). The greatest oil-producing countries of the world belong to the Arabs who also are the descendants of Abraham. Nevertheless, God said the Patriarch would be blessed through the seed of Isaac, and that meant the Hebrews, the nation of Israel. Apart from this fact, the ancient promise has already been fulfilled. If the promise refers to Israel, then the Jews must either extend their borders, or oil must be found within their present territory.

"The Middle East is a region that supplies at least 70% of the oil consumed daily by non-communist countries. It is the source of well over 50% of West Europe's oil; 90% of Japan's; 30% of the U.S.A.'s; and 80% of Africa's. Every fifteen minutes a tanker filled with oil sails through the Strait of Hormuz at the head of the Persian Gulf, enroute to oil refineries around the world" (*The Encyclopedia of Illustrations*, Dr. Paul Lee Tan, p. 797, Assurance Publishers, Rockville, Maryland). It is now recognized that Sodom and Gomorrah were destroyed by an oil fire resulting from an earthquake which devastated the area around the Dead Sea. Some years ago a Jewish business man named Federman expressed the belief that oil had returned to the region, and efforts were made to begin Israel's first oil exploration. Unfortunately, his efforts were unsuccessful. A prominent television broadcaster in California announced in June, 1989, that oil had been found near one of Israel's cities. The world is waiting to see if his statements are accurate. When Israel becomes a great oil producing nation, her importance in world affairs will increase enormously. The use of tankers to transport oil from foreign ports will become unnecessary; Israel would export oil from her own Mediterranean terminals. Danger will also increase, for her Middle East neighbors will envy her prosperity. This might be the time in history when the promise made by Moses to Zebulun will be fulfilled.

"For I know that my redeemer liveth, and that he shall stand at the latter day upon the earth. And though after my skin worms destroy this body, yet in my flesh shall I see God; Whom I shall see for myself, and mine eyes shall behold, and not another" (Job 19:25–27).

To repeat what has already been said, the writing of Job is believed to be the first biblical book written. It belonged to a period when the earth was comparatively young. There was no recognized house of God; few, if any, prophets; no Scripture; and no religious institution to which Job could have appealed for enlightenment. The patriarch lived in an era when theological conception was in its infancy, and it was therefore remarkable that during his suffering he developed amazing ideas. His increasing perception of survival was seen in three statements: (a) how dismal—death was the end of all things (see Job 3:11–17); (b) how doubtful —he asked a question, "If a man die, shall he live again?" (Job 14:14); and (c) how decided—"For I know that my redeemer liveth, and that he shall stand at the latter day upon the earth" (Job 19:25). Some writers deny there was any prophetical value in these texts, but for evangelical students Job's testimony remains one of the most inspiring utterances in ancient literature (see the author's book, *Bible Cameos*, pp. 69–70).

His Glowing Certainty . . . *"I Know"*

Surrounded by circumstances and people who encouraged doubt, Job's faith was resplendent. Although his friends believed he was a hypocrite, and his wife advised him to curse God and die, Job's testimony was a light shining in darkness. He did not understand why he was suffering such anguish; he did not appreciate the comments of his neighbors, but he remained sure of the integrity of God. It was this fact which enabled him to exclaim, "But he knoweth the way that I take: when he hath tried me, I shall come forth as gold" (Job 23:10).

His Gracious Colleague . . . *My Redeemer*

Even in antiquity the function of the *goel* or "redeemer" was well-known. He was a kinsman who possessed the authority to redeem slaves or property, a man who intervened when misfortune overtook a relative. Job believed God to be a near kinsman, that in some mysterious way, He was closely related and cared sufficiently to help His family. Job was a man who saw and believed truth yet to be revealed.

His Great Claim . . . *Liveth*

How Job arrived at his conclusion is open to conjecture. He had been in "the refiner's fire," and maybe his revelation came from God who superintended operations. His earlier contention that death terminated existence stood out in bold relief. If all else died, God remained immortal; His everlasting love for human beings could not diminish.

His Growing Confidence . . . *"He Shall Stand at the Latter Day upon the Earth"*

Serious thinkers would never deny this was partially fulfilled when the Son of God came to earth to redeem sinners. Nevertheless, the remaining part of the text suggests even more. Job went on to say, "Yet in my flesh shall I see God." Although Job endured his misfortunes and came through his ordeal triumphantly, his ultimate decease was inevitable. The decaying process could not be prevented, but Job declared, "And though . . . worms destroy this body, yet in my flesh shall I see God." Job believed his mortal body would put on immortality, that the corruptible would put on incorruption. His vision embraced eternity, and therefore his utterance must be included among those promises awaiting fulfillment. It is difficult to decide whence came such knowledge. Perhaps it would be safe to assume he was taught by the Lord Himself.

His Glorious Conclusion . . . *"Whom I Shall See for Myself"*

Evidently Job's faith removed the fear of death. In some delightful way God revealed Himself to His trusting servant, and the patriarch believed he had received a promise of immortality. He would die, but the Lord would raise him from the dead and provide a glorified body. He would stand with his divine Redeemer upon the earth. This realization enabled him to say, as did Paul, "O death, where is thy sting? O grave, where is thy victory?" (1 Cor. 15:55). The prolonged trial of Job revealed two things: (a) increased riches which could not prolong his life; and (b) a triumphant faith which money could not buy. Which was the greater?

"For, behold, I create new heavens and a new earth: and the former shall not be remembered, nor come into mind . . . And I will rejoice in Jerusalem, and joy in my people . . . There shall be no more thence an infant of days, nor an old man that hath not filled his days: for the child shall die an hundred years old" (Isa. 65:17–20). "And everything shall live whither the river cometh" (Ezek. 47:9).

Disease has always been one of man's greatest enemies, and throughout time gifted men struggled to overcome its supremacy. One of the first licensed physicians was Imhotep, an Egyptian, who practiced medicine about 3,000 B.C. He was very successful, and Egyptians worshiped him as a god. Originally, physicians were priests, and their medicines were the result of mingled faith and superstition. As their knowledge increased, some doctors became surgeons, and the embalming of bodies became a practiced art (see Gen. 50:2). The first female obstetricians mentioned in the Bible were Shiphrah and Puah, who saved the lives of many Hebrew children (see Ex. 1:15–17).

"About 300 B.C. a famous school of medicine was started in Alexandria, Egypt. The faculty had the benefit of considerable medical knowledge from Greek, Roman, Babylonian and Indian sources. It is wise for Bible students to remember this. If Luke were trained at the Alexandrian school, or by graduates of that school, his medical knowledge had considerable scientific basis" (*The Zondervan Pictorial Encyclopedia of the Bible*, p. 788).

The method used by Jesus was different from those of all other medical practitioners. He never gave prescriptions, but issued His word of command. He spoke, and sufferers were healed. Yet, apart from a few special occasions, death remained an unassailable foe. Today doctors only delay the inevitable. Perhaps that explains the strenuous efforts now being made to increase longevity. Some people, suffering from terminal illness submit to experiments whereby their bodies are frozen after death and preserved, to be restored at a later date when cures have been found for their ailments. It is apparent, however, that medical research has its limitations, and even famous people die.

Against this background of human effort and failure, the words of Isaiah shine as a beacon light. He also had limited knowledge of medicine and advised that a plaster of figs be placed upon the body of his dying king (see Isa. 38:21). As the prophet looked down the corridor of time, he saw the desired breakthrough of medical research. Nevertheless, he explained the ultimate triumph would only come when God performed a miracle. The prophet wrote, "The child shall die an hundred years old, but the sinner being an hundred years old shall be accursed" (Isa. 65:20).

That prediction suggested many ideas. If death at the age of one hundred years were to be considered the life span of a child, then how old would the parents be? They could possibly live for seven, eight, or more hundreds of years. That would mean a revolutionary change in the mortality rate. Major diseases such as cancer will be overcome; other threats to human life will be nonexistent, and hospitals and morticians may be inactive. Yet this can only happen when Christ reigns upon the earth. Ezekiel endorsed Zechariah's account of the great earthquake which will divide the Mount of Olives; he predicted its activity would release from the earth a river of water possessing medicinal curatives. He said, "Everything shall live whither the river cometh" (Ezek. 47:9). The people who journey to Jerusalem to worship the King of Kings will find refreshment for their souls in the sanctuary and healing for their bodies in the river of life. God's ultimate aim is the complete elimination of death. Paul wrote of the end times, "For he must reign, till he hath put all enemies under his feet. The last enemy that shall be destroyed is death" (1 Cor. 15:25–26).

Faith and science should walk together. Talented men who seek for new cures need God's help. Behind each new discovery is the smiling face of the Almighty. When the greatest efforts of men fail, He can perform what is impossible by any other means. This was demonstrated during the ministry of Christ. The possibilities will be boundless when He reigns in righteousness over all the kingdoms of the earth.

"Moreover I . . . will set my sanctuary in the midst of them forever- more. My tabernacle also shall be with them: yea, I will be their God, and they shall be my people" (Ezek. 37:26–27).

Whether or not a new temple will be erected in Jerusalem has caused endless discussion in theological circles. There are three schools of thought regarding the message of Ezekiel: (a) He predict- ed a rebuilding of Solomon's temple after the Babylonian captivity; (b) He was prophesying about the Church in a figurative sense; and (c) A still future, literal temple will be built during the millennial kingdom.

The first suggestion is unacceptable because the temple restored after the captivity was not erected according to the specifications given by Ezekiel. Furthermore, it did not last forever. The second idea presents problems. If the prophet were merely describing a hypothetical idea, why did he waste time supplying irrelevant mea- surements? The Savior said, "When ye therefore shall see the abom- ination of desolation, spoken of by Daniel the prophet, stand in the holy place . . . Then let them which be in Judaea flee into the mountains" (Matt. 24:15–16). These details mention geographical positions. The Jews believe that when their Messiah arrives, a mag- nificent temple will be erected as evidence of the covenant to be made with His people.

This interpretation begets another problem. The Bible teaches the Antichrist will make an agreement with Israel guaranteeing po- litical and religious independence for seven years. Unfortunately, "in the midst of the week" (see Dan. 9:27), he will violate the agreement and "cause the sacrifice and the oblation to cease." Theo- logians differ in their doctrines concerning the return of Christ, but they agree that the desecration of the holy place will take place *before* the millennial reign. Therefore, the temple either in part or the whole, must be constructed prior to the return of the Messiah.

The Israelis are the most heavily taxed people on earth. Their military expenses are astronomical, and without foreign aid such an enterprise cannot be considered. It has also been claimed the Mosque of Omar stands upon the site of the ancient temple. Since Jews would not build elsewhere, it will need to be demolished. One rabbi said, "That presents no problem—God could send an earthquake!"

The majority of Jews in modern Israel are not religiously inclined; many are professed athiests. During a visit to the Holy Land, I asked a Hebrew guide a question concerning God and the holocaust in Germany. He became sarcastic, saying, "Bah! We Jews are supposed to be God's chosen people. He must have been asleep when six million of us perished in the gas ovens of Hitler's Germany. Sir, if that is the way God looks after His people, we prefer to look after ourselves!" Unfortunately, many Israeli citizens would agree with his statement. On the other hand, devout Jews are struggling to restore faith in God and the complete restoration of everything relative to Old Testament customs.

Dr. Paul Lee Tan has said, "A special school has been established in Israel to train young Israelis of the tribe of Levi in ancient rites of sacrifice. It is called 'Yeshiva Avodas Hakodesh' The school was founded by Rabbi Hirsh Ha-Cohen, and dedicated in December 1970. Only students who can trace their ancestry to Aaron are admitted. There they learn the laws of ancient animal sacrifice and how to perform the practices which existed in the ancient temple" *(Encyclopedia of Illustrations*, p. 634, Assurance Publishers, Rockville, MD).

Unfortunately, certain speakers make statements which cannot be verified. Rumors of stones made to specification and sent from America to Israel have spread through the world. Indignant denials have been made by the Israeli authorities, but people are wondering what and whom to believe. If financial burdens were lifted from the Jewish nation, the building of the temple could easily be arranged. American Jews alone could, and probably would, underwrite the expense necessary for the fulfillment of Israel's greatest project. Oral Roberts, in his book *End Times*, reports a statement made during his conversation with the late Prime Minister of Israel, David Ben Gurion. He said, "We are not a religious people, but we need our temple to bind us all together." As the plans of God continue to unfold, events will become increasingly dramatic.

> Nearer and nearer draws the time:
> The time that shall surely be
> When the earth shall be filled with the glory of God
> As the waters cover the sea.

"Thus saith the Lord God; Behold, O my people, I will open your graves, and cause you to come up out of your graves, and bring you into the land of Israel . . . And shall put my spirit in you, and ye shall live, and I shall place you in your own land: then shall ye know that I the LORD have spoken it, and performed it, saith the LORD" (Ezek. 37:12, 14).

The thirty-seventh chapter of Ezekiel is one of the most sensational messages ever written; what the prophet predicted nearly 3,000 years ago is now being fulfilled. The young priest was explicit when he wrote, "The hand of the LORD was upon me, and carried me out in the spirit of the LORD, and set me down in the midst of the valley which was full of bones, and caused me to pass by them round about: and, behold, there were very many in the open valley; and lo, they were very dry" (Ezek. 37:1–2).

The Holy Spirit conducted Ezekiel on a walking tour through a cemetery! Skeletons were everywhere. When the prophet saw a mass movement of bones, he was probably shocked and wondered if he were dreaming. Then God explained this was a preview of what He intended to accomplish. His explanation was clear and concise. The bones represented the Hebrews who had been scattered around the world. The Lord intended to change that situation; He would regather the people and make them a nation within their own land. This promise was partially fulfilled when the captives returned from Babylon, but at that time Jews only returned from Babylon. The *complete* fulfillment of God's promise has yet to take place. The prophet said, "And they shall dwell in the land that I have given unto Jacob my servant . . . and they shall dwell therein, even they, and their children, and their children's children *forever*; and my servant David shall be their prince for ever" (Ezek. 37:25).

Disturbing the Dead . . . *A Tremendous Miracle*

"So I prophesied as I was commanded: and as I prophesied, there was a noise, and behold a shaking, and the bones came together, bone to his bone . . . and the breath came into them, and they lived, and stood up upon their feet, an exceeding great army" (Ezek. 37:7–10). The miracle of the dead bones was astonishing, but evidently God's prediction was even more astounding. Israel had been the greatest nation on earth, but the Babylonian captivity obliterated her magnificence. Although the edict of Cyrus enabled many of the captives to return to Palestine, others refused to accept his offer. That was the beginning of a dispersion which carried Jews to every part of the earth. Centuries later, the Romans destroyed Jerusalem, and the people lost their national home. They were expelled from many countries and persecuted unmercifully. The sufferers had no government to which to appeal for assistance; their future was bleak. Then suddenly, the question "Can these bones live?" assumed a new meaning, and it became evident nothing was too difficult for God to accomplish.

Dispelling the Doubts . . . *A Thrilling Message*

The Psalmist said, "Surely the wrath of man shall praise thee: the remainder of wrath shalt thou restrain" (Ps. 76:10). The Lord possessed the amazing ability to accomplish the impossible. This became evident during the lifetime of Hitler, when in spite of the murder of millions of Jews, displaced Hebrews began to dream of returning to their homeland. The dead bones of Israel's nationalism began to move, and ultimately, God made them to stand "in their own land." Not long ago there were no Jews in Jerusalem, and very few in the entire land of Palestine. Today, there are between four and five million, and the number is steadily increasing. Harry Golden wrote in the *Holiday* magazine, "The minimum requirement to immigrate into Israel is the statement, 'I am a Jew.' The immigrant needs no papers, no testimonials, no affidavits signed by rabbis, and no religious tests. Here, for the first time, immigrants may come into a country where they are not punctured by needles nor forced to display their teeth."

Describing the Deliverer . . . *A Trusted Monarch*

When this movement was in its infancy, Prime Minister Ben-Gurion said, "Our policy is to bring all Jews to Israel . . . we are still at the beginning." This continues, and the most sensational events are yet to occur. "And I will set up one shepherd over them, and he shall feed them, even my servant David . . . And I the LORD will be their God, and my servant David a prince among them; I the LORD have spoken it" (Ezek. 34:23–24). "and my servant David shall be their prince for ever" (Ezek. 37:25). Evidently, these promises have never been fulfilled. God has brought His people from all parts of the earth, and will complete what He commenced.

153

"Now let them put away their whoredom, and the carcases of their kings, far from me, and I will dwell in the midst of them for ever" (Ezek. 43:9).

Ezekiel was reared in Jerusalem, and probably was a priest when he was taken with other captives to Babylon. He ministered to Israel throughout the captivity, and methods used in the presentation of his message, were, to say the least, sensational. He drew a plan of Jerusalem on a brick (see 4:1–3). He lay on one side of his body for several days, and then on the other (see 4:4–8). He shaved himself with a sword, and then divided the hair (see 5:1–17). His methods were extremely effective, for at all times the prophet explained the reasons for his strange behavior. He mentioned the possibility of God's residing in Jerusalem forever.

God Resided with Adam and Eve . . . *For Days*

It was written, "And they heard the voice of the LORD God walking in the garden in the cool of the day" (Gen. 3:8). The Lord desired communion with the man and woman He had created, and that could have continued eternally. Unfortunately, sin ruined the happiness of our first parents and changed the plans of the Almighty. Distance replaced the warm, thrilling fellowship of those early days, and Adam and Eve were expelled from their garden. God did not forsake His children, but the glowing ecstasy of the initial happiness was overshadowed by human guilt. Nevertheless, the Lord never lost the desire to live among His people.

God Resided with Israel . . . *For Forty Years*

God's people have never been expected to walk alone! When the Lord brought Israel out of Egypt, He accompanied them throughout their wilderness journeys. Realizing their inability to see an invisible God, He commanded Moses to erect a tabernacle and arranged that a cloud should be above it by day, and a pillar of fire by night. These were indications that the Lord would be in residence among His people. The same truth was evident when the glory of God filled Solomon's temple. Alas, the sign of God's presence was removed, and the wayward Israelites became captives in Babylon.

The Savior Resided with People . . . *During His Lifetime*

It is impossible to describe adequately the magnificence of the Lord's ministry, for His miracles were shared only with men and women in Palestine. Yet, for those who were privileged to be present, children on on His knee, lepers being cleansed—and joy shining in His eyes—were evidence that God had not changed. He loved being with His children. That delightful characteristic remained unchanged from the earliest days of time.

The Spirit Resides In The Church . . . *Until The End Of The Age*

The abiding presence of the Holy Spirit is probably the greatest asset of Christians. The Old Testament revealed that God was *for* His people; the Gospels explained how God was *with* His disciples; the remaining part of the New Testament taught that God was *in* His followers. However wonderful these facts appear to be, they fall short of what God promised. The Holy Spirit lives within the church, but unfortunately, human weakness often hides Him from those whose vision is limited.

God Will Reside in Jerusalem . . . *Forever*!

It is thrilling to remember that when Israel's iniquity has been removed, and when the City of David becomes what it should always have been, the Lord will live in His temple, and everybody will know He is God. At that time people will worship Him in Jerusalem and observe the Feast of Tabernacles. They will know God is in their midst (see Zech. 14:16). Time will not terminate His residency. Throughout eternal ages the Lord and His people will be united.

If a text may be quoted out of its setting, then exultantly it can be said, "Eye hath not seen, nor ear heard, neither have entered into the heart of man, the things which God hath prepared for them that love him" (1 Cor. 2:9). Then, as never before, other predictions will be fulfilled. "Thus saith the LORD of hosts; In those days it shall come to pass, that ten men shall take hold out of all languages of the nations, even shall take hold of the skirt of him that is a Jew, saying, We will go with you: for we have heard that God is with you" (Zech. 8:23).

"Therefore, behold, I will allure her, and bring her into the wilderness, and speak comfortably unto her. And I will give her vineyards from thence, and the valley of Achor for a door of hope: and she shall sing there, as in the days of her youth, and as in the day when she came up out of the land of Egypt" (Hos. 2:14–15).

One of the most delightful flowers in the world is only found in Western Australia where it blossoms beneath the ground. A complete specimen has never been found, for in the vast expanse of the desert, it is impossible to know where to find it. Farmers who farm adjacent lands sometimes find broken pieces of the rare plant. Plows cut the flower in pieces, and these are thrown to the surface. Businessmen in Perth published an artist's impression of the flower, and if the real thing resembles what has been imagined, it is among the most beautiful orchids in existence. Yet, it blooms in the dark!

The prophet Hosea would have appreciated that fact. His marital affairs produced one of the strangest stories in the Scripture. The popular young preacher married a lady of ill-repute who eventually deserted her family to rejoin former lovers. Misfortune followed her, and unable to pay her debts, she was offered for sale at a slave auction (see the author's book *Bible Gems*, pp. 63–64, Kregel Publications, Grand Rapids, MI). The prophet mentioned his wife when he spoke to Israel and made a remarkable statement. He described a vineyard in a wilderness and the finding of treasure in a most unlikely place. Hosea assured his listeners that as he had forgiven and restored his spouse, God was willing to do the same things for His wife, Israel. He would always be willing to do this if they would destroy their idols.

The references to "vineyards in the wilderness" and "the valley of Achor as a door of hope" invite investigation. The former suggests fruitfulness in a desert, and the latter, hope where there was only despair. Achan had committed an unpardonable sin when he secretly stole prohibited articles. His body had been buried beneath a pile of stones in "the valley of Achor" (see Josh. 7). Thereafter, the place and its name became a curse in Israel. Yet God indicated the desolate area could become an entrance into a new realm of blessedness.

To be taken into the wilderness would normally suggest God intended to punish his erring children. Nevertheless, in this instance

He promised to speak comfortably to His people. The cloud of God's judgment had a silver lining. Occasionally, very precious things are discovered in a desert, especially when God becomes a Guide!

God's Message Is Always Sympathetic . . . *"I Will Speak Comfortably"*

Sometimes, God thought it necessary to chastise His people, but gentleness always held the rod! Even in the final days of time when Israel endures unprecedented anguish, God intends to deliver a remnant of his people. Even their place of barrenness will become an avenue of hope, leading to the magnificent splendor of Christ's reign upon earth.

God's Majesty Is Permanently Supreme . . . *"I Will Give Her"*

The end of God's work can never be in doubt! Evil may appear to win occasional battles, but the ultimate triumph of righteousness is assured. God is supreme, His word infallible, and His power unlimited. Whatever He plans comes to pass. The church knows it, Israel will know it, and every Christian should rejoice and "abide under the shadow of the Almighty" (see Ps. 91:1).

God's Mercy Is Frequently Surprising . . . *"I Will Give Her Vineyards"*

"The valley of Achor for a door of hope." God promised to make the unattractive, frightening valley of judgment become a path to unsurpassed happiness. He alone was able to accomplish a miracle of that caliber. Where stones had fallen in judgment, benedictions would descend in grace. The kindness of the Lord would turn tears to laughter, mourning to rejoicing, and despair into everlasting hope. These brief promises are cameos revealing the expanding grace of the Almighty.

God's Music Is Constantly Sublime . . . *"She Shall Sing . . . "*

"She shall sing there, as in the days of her youth, and as in the day when she came up out of the land of Egypt." When Israel left Egypt and discovered the Lord's ability to divide the Red Sea, cares vanished, fear disappeared, and their music probably filled angels with delight. No man can be rescued from a horrible pit without desiring to sing a new song (see Ps. 40:1–3).

"And his feet shall stand in that day upon the mount of Olives, which is before Jerusalem on the east, and the mount of Olives shall cleave in the midst thereof toward the east and toward the west, and there shall be a very great valley; and half of the mountain shall remove toward the north, and half of it toward the south" (Zech. 14:4).

Earthquakes have always terrorized mankind; to stand amid swaying and falling buildings when ground movements resemble the waves of the sea is a frightening experience. Men may be educated or illiterate, rich or poor, important or ordinary individuals, but when the earth shakes and mountains shudder, everyone becomes helpless. It has been claimed that one of the most disastrous quakes in history occurred in 1556 in Shensi, Central China, when 650,000 people died and approximately 780,000 were injured. These astounding figures make the human spirit tremble.

The U.S. government has spent enormous sums of money on earthquake research hoping to obtain information that would warn of approaching catastrophies in time to save many lives. Stringent building laws have been applied to new constructions, and the seismologists work ceaselessly to discover means of accurately predicting such catastrophies. Unfortunately, their reports have been inconclusive.

The Unique Prediction . . . *A Devastating Eruption*

Zechariah, the prophet, was born in Babylon and returned with Ezra and Nehemiah to Palestine. When he was still a younge man, God ordained him to become a prophet. He had no academic ability and had never graduated from a college. Yet, in a remarkable way, he described events to take place thousands of years after his death. Apart from divine enabling, it would have been impossible for that young man to utter his statements. The Middle Eastern countries have often been troubled by earthquakes, but the Mount of Olives has never been rent apart. It is known that a major earthquake fault exists beneath the mountain (see the author's book *"What in the World Will Happen Next?"*, page 133, Kregel Publications, Grand Rapids, MI). The evidence of a true prophet was his ability to disclose details unknown to other people. God put words into His servant's mouth that they might be relayed to a national audience.

The Unavoidable Power . . . *A Detailed Explanation*

The details of the expected earthquake in Israel are exciting. The prophet said the mountain would be divided; one half would move to the north and the other to the south to create a valley between the seas. The prophet Isaiah supplied extra details. He said low places will be exalted and high places brought low (see Isa. 40:4). God's mighty power will make a valley between the Mediterranean and Dead seas. The Salt Sea will be exalted, and Jerusalem lowered to make the city of David a seaport. During the reign of Christ upon the earth, ships will be able to take their pilgrim passengers all the way to their desired destination.

An illustration of what will happen may be found in the Corinthian Canal which was completed in 1893 across the isthmus of Corinth. The emperor Nero initiated such a construction in 78 A.D. but later abandoned his project. Thereafter, vessels were frequently pulled on wooden rollers across the isthmus. Engineers completed the waterway in 1893, and their achievement is now admired annually by millions of tourists. God will miraculously create another canal from the "Great Sea" to the "Salt Sea."

The Unlimited Possessions . . . *A Decided Eruption*

It would be impossible to overemphasize the far-reaching effects of the eruption that will change the appearance of Israel. Dr. Paul Lee Tan stated, "The wealth of the Dead Sea is so enormous as to be almost unbelievable. . . . After Jerusalem was captured in 1917 by General Allenby, a British geologist began to investigate the mineral riches of the Dead Sea. And the secret has come out. Its tremendous reserve is estimated at 22 thousand million tons of magnesium chloride; 12 thousand million tons of common salt; 6 thousand million tons of calcium chloride; and 1 thousand million tons of magnesium bromide. The saleable value of these chemicals would come out at the staggering figure of $1,270,000,000,000. This amount would be equal to the combined wealth of the United States, Great Britain, France, Germany and Italy" (see *Encyclopedia of Illustrations*, p. 627, Assurance Publishers, Rockville, MD). When the hand of God stirs that entire region and riches buried deep in the earth are brought to the surface, Israel's wealth will be beyond calculation.

> *"Then they that feared the LORD spake often one to another: and the LORD hearkened, and heard it, and a book of remembrance was written before him for them that feared the LORD, and that thought upon his name. And they shall be mine, saith the LORD of hosts, in that day when I make up my jewels" (Mal. 3:16–17).*

Malachi was a prophet commissioned by God to help Nehemiah in the task of restoring Jerusalem. The reformer, returning from Babylon, discovered corruption among the priests and people. The burden of caring for and leading the nation became too heavy for one man to carry. The prophet became a source of unfailing strength to his leader. He not only rebuked the compromising men in the temple, but he also encouraged faithful people. In spite of the apostasy which had ruined the nation, some remained true to the Lord and His laws (see the author's book *Bible Gems*, pp. 91–92, Kregel Publications, Grand Rapids, MI).

God's Inspired People. . . *"They That Feared the Lord"*

Nehemiah was encouraged to know that throughout the land were men and women who detested the actions of their religious leaders. They met at various locations to converse about the goodness of the Lord, and the Lord was pleased with their conversations. The word "often" should be emphasized; the people met and worshiped as often as they were able. At a much later time, the Savior referred to similar people as "the salt of the earth." They were wise. Paul would have appreciated them, for he said, "Whatsoever things are lovely . . . think on these things" (Phil. 4:8).

God's Important Purpose . . . *"A Book of Remembrance Was Written"*

The book of remembrance was written, not to help God remember, but so that its existence would encourage the faithful to strive for even greater triumphs. Angels are interested in the affairs of earth and rejoice when people respond to the claims of Christ (see Luke 15:10). Evidently God's country is nearer to ours than some people imagine. *The Living Bible* translates Hebrews 12:1 as, "Since we have such a huge crowd of men of faith, watching us from the grandstands, let us strip off anything that slows us down, or holds us back."

God's Invaluable Property ... "*My Jewels*"

God spoke of the time when He would make up His jewels. A better translation would be "when I display my special treasure." It is not known when this will take place. This is one of the unfulfilled promises of the Bible. Many people collect stamps, coins, works of art, or diamonds and other jewels which are very valuable. The Lord also has a collection of jewels which He purchased with His precious blood (see 1 Peter 1:18–19). The Savior is proud of His treasures and according to the text intends to display them before the assembled hosts of heaven. To be present at that display and to be a part of that unique treasure will be a privilege beyond comprehension. It has been claimed that one redeemed soul is worth more than the world. Perhaps the Savior's evaluation would be even higher. He believed that to obtain such a treasure, it was worth dying on the cross.

God's Immense Protection ... "*And They Shall Be Mine*"

To protect their treasures, owners do amazing things. Diamonds are placed in vaults. Works of art are displayed in museums patrolled by guards, and even stamps and coins are carefully guarded. Collectors are pleased with their acquisitions and are proud of their possessions. Evidently the Savior has similar feelings. Sometimes, His diamonds have flaws, but with the skill of an expert, He works on the blemishes. It is thrilling to know that when He shall appear, we shall be like Him (see 1 John 3:1–2).

God's Inexhaustible Power ... "*I Will Spare Them ...*"

Malachi evidently believed God's judgments would overtake the false priests whose evil example had influenced the nation. Yet he predicted the Lord would protect His faithful servants. He compared an earthly parent with God, and his definition was new. The fatherhood of God was something which Jesus taught. Perhaps the prophet was preparing the way for the new concept. The Lord was not one to be feared but loved. The continuing affection for His jewels guaranteed He would never forget them.

"Ye men of Galilee, why stand ye gazing up into heaven? this same Jesus, which is taken up from you into heaven, shall so come in like manner as ye have seen him go into heaven" (Acts 1:11).

It was a solemn but delightful moment! The Lord had delivered His final message and had ascended into the heavens. The disciples watched His homegoing; one moment He was with them, the next He was gone. It could not be true, and yet it was! They were like men in a trance; then nearby voices aroused them. "Ye men of Galilee, why stand ye gazing up into heaven?"

The late Dr. G. Campbell Morgan believed the two messengers were Moses and Elijah. He suggested that angels were always called "angels," hence the "two men clothed in white apparel" must have been human! His deduction is questionable for angels were sometimes called "men" (see Josh. 5:13; Mark 16:5). The interpretation is inconsequential because the message far exceeds the importance of the messengers. The angels were convinced of certain details.

The Disciples Were Sure of His Destination . . . *Heaven*

When Elijah was taken up by a whirlwind into heaven (see 2 Kings 2:11), the sons of the prophets which were at Jericho said, "Behold now, there be with thy servants fifty strong men; let them go, we pray thee, and seek thy master: lest peradventure the Spirit of the LORD hath taken him up, and cast him upon some mountain, or into some valley. And he (Elisha) said, Ye shall not send. And when they urged him till he was ashamed, he said, Send. They sent therefore fifty men; and they sought three days, but found him not" (2 Kings 2:16–17).

The angels who spoke to the disciples had no such illusions. They knew where Christ had gone, and realized the importance of His mission. The writer to the Hebrews expressed the same truth, "For Christ is not entered into the holy places made with hands . . . but into heaven itself, now to appear in the presence of God for us" (Heb. 9:24). The angels who had rejoiced at Christ's birth and witnessed to His resurrection knew that since the earthly phase of His work had been completed, the heavenly ministry was just beginning. He was to become the representative of His people before the throne of God. The disciples should not be gazing at clouds when there was much work to be done.

They Were Sure of His Determination . . . *To Return to Earth*

"This same Jesus . . . shall so come." There was nothing new about the message, for the Savior had enunciated identical facts. He would be as a nobleman going into a far country but would certainly return. The Lord urged His followers to be diligent during His absence (see Luke 19:12–13). Throughout His ministry Christ repeatedly affirmed that the establishing of God's kingdom would be linked more with His second coming. He came first to redeem sinners; He promised to come again to claim those who responded to the Gospel. Jesus said, "And if I go and prepare a place for you, I will come again, and receive you unto myself; that where I am, there ye may be also" (John 14:3).

The angels were well-informed. They were aware of God's plans and helped to fulfill His purposes. They assured the disciples that Christ would return "in like manner, as ye have seen him go into heaven." That promise has never been fulfilled. It was true when the Holy Spirit descended at Pentecost, but that did not fulfill what had been promised. He went up with a body which could be seen and handled (see 1 John 1:1). Furthermore, He ascended from the Mount of Olives to which, according to the prophet Zechariah, He will return (see Zech. 14:4). If there be any meaning in the Bible, Christ must come back to earth.

They Were Sure of His Durability . . . *"In Like Manner"*

The angels promised that Christ would be seen "in like manner, as ye have seen him go into heaven." That statement was an affirmation of immortality and evidence that the glorious body of the Savior would be ageless, unchanging, and enduring. Even though almost 2,000 years would pass, the Lord would be unaltered. His face, hands, side, and general appearance would be the same. The prophet Zechariah said, "And one shall say unto him, What are these wounds in thine hands? Then he shall answer, Those with which I was wounded in the house of my friends (Zech. 13:6). That prediction has never been fulfilled. The time must come when the Lord will return in the clouds of heaven to be seen and heard by millions of people. Paul wrote, "That at the name of Jesus, every knee should bow . . . and that every tongue should confess that Jesus Christ is Lord, to the glory of God the Father" (Phil. 2:10–11). The angels were correct when they said, "The kingdoms of this world are become the kingdoms of our Lord, and of His Christ" (Rev. 11:15). "And they shall see his face" (Rev. 22:4).

THE PROMISE THAT IS THE HOPE OF THE CHURCH

"Looking for that blessed hope, and the glorious appearing of the great God and our Savior Jesus Christ" (Titus 2:13).

Webster's Dictionary defines hope as "confidence in a future event; the highest degree of well-founded expectation of good." Hope is a golden thread to be seen in all parts of the Bible; it is a diamond with brilliant facets and appears at least forty-eight times in the New Testament. The apostle Peter wrote, "Blessed be the God and Father of our Lord Jesus Christ, which according to his abundant mercy hath begotten us again unto a lively (living) hope by the resurrection of Jesus Christ from the dead" (1 Peter 1:3). Peter believed hope was an important by-product of regeneration, a fountain of living water arising within the soul to overcome doubt and banish despair.

A Saving Hope . . . *How Redemptive*

"For we are saved by hope: but hope that is seen is not hope: for what a man seeth, why doth he yet hope for?" (Rom. 8:24). A man does not hope for something already in his possession. Rejoicing in what he has, he anticipates more! Salvation, the forgiveness of sin and everlasting life are gifts of God's grace, but the hope of the church is to be saved from sin's presence. Whatever Christians have received, it is nothing compared with what God has in store for them. It is difficult for a true believer to be completely satisfied upon the earth. He looks for "a city which hath foundations, whose builder and maker is God" (Heb. 11:10).

A Sure Hope . . . *How Reliable*

"Which hope we have as an anchor of the soul, both sure and stedfast, and which entereth into that within the veil" (Heb. 6:19). The writer of this letter was careful to indicate that "strong consolation" was something acquired by those "who fled for refuge" to Christ. The same kind of word was used for those who went to the cities of refuge in Israel A good anchor never drifted. Evidently, a man's faith in Christ should endure at all times.

A Splendid Hope . . . *How Reassuring*

"Blessed be the God and Father of our Lord Jesus Christ, which . . . hath begotten us again unto a lively hope by the resurrection of Jesus Christ from the dead" (1 Peter 1:3). Whatever hope the believer possessed prior to his regeneration, it increased greatly after his conversion to Christ. Peter mentioned "an inheritance incorruptible, and undefiled, and that fadeth not away, reserved in heaven for you" (1 Peter 1:4). The apostle's words covered a wide span from bankruptcy to benevolence, from rags to riches, from unashamed wickedness to unlimited wealth. That hope thrilled the soul and provided the encouragement needed to live triumphantly.

A Special Hope . . . *How Remarkable*

"Now our Lord Jesus Christ himself, and God, even our Father, which hath loved us, and hath given us everlasting consolation and and good hope through grace" (2 Thess. 2:16). God always gives lavishly; there are no strings to His offers and no time limit to deprive people of their possessions in Christ. Everlasting life is followed by everlasting consolation. Looking back leads to regret; to look ahead is to rejoice. A good hope is unquestionably encouraging; it can never be false, and it cannot be denied.

A Sanctifying Hope . . . *How Rewarding*

"But we know that, when he shall appear, we shall be like him; for we shall see him as he is. And every man that hath this hope in him purifieth himself, even as he is pure" (1 John 3:2–3). As brides anticipate pleasing their bridegrooms, so Christians yearn for the Marriage of the Lamb. To love Christ is to desire to please Him. Purification is not automatic; it demands effort, and a deliberate renunciation.

A Soothing Hope . . . *How Reviving*

"That ye sorrow not, even as others which have no hope. For if we believe that Jesus died and rose again, even so them also which sleep in Jesus will God bring with him. . . . Wherefore comfort one another with these words" (1 Thess. 4:13–14, 18). Paul believed saints who died were absent from the body, and present with the Lord (see 2 Cor. 5:8). He explained that believers will possess bodies "like unto Christ's glorious body" (Phil. 3:21). When the Savior returns, the mortal will put on immortality and glorified saints will live in new bodies forever. Paul believed that message was a cure for broken hearts!

"For this we say unto you by the word of the Lord, that we which are alive and remain unto the coming of the Lord shall not prevent them which are asleep. For the Lord himself shall descend from heaven with a shout, with the voice of the archangel, and with the trump of God: and the dead in Christ shall rise first: Then we which are alive and remain shall be caught up together with them in the clouds, to meet the Lord in the air: and so shall we ever be with the Lord" (1 Thess. 4:15–17).

When the Lord instructed His disciples concerning the forthcoming ministry of the Holy Spirit, He said, "Howbeit when he, the Spirit of truth, is come, he will guide you into all truth" (John 16:13). Nevertheless, Christ did not promise this would be accomplished instantaneously. Sometimes, illumination and understanding come in a moment; at others, the learning process is developed gradually.

Luke, in describing the death of Stephen, said, "He fell asleep" (Acts 7:60). The beloved physician used the word *koimaomai* which is found 18 times in the New Testament. It refers to slumber or taking of a rest in sleep. It is used in John 11:13 in reference to the death of Lazarus. The early Christians considered death to be falling into a deep sleep from which they would awaken in the Resurrection. Nevertheless, being asleep did not mean they were dead! Paul progressed in his understanding of truth.

Deep Sleep . . . *Restricting*

When David died, it was written, "So David slept with his fathers, and was buried in the city of David" (1 Kings 2:10). Egyptians believed in another world; their kings and queens were buried with many articles thought to be needed on the journey to the hereafter. The Hebrews were different. They considered death to be a place of inactivity where the deceased slumbered with ancestors.

The idea of life beyond the tomb was undeveloped, and even during the ministry of Jesus the Sadducees denied the possibility of a future existence, believing death meant separation, inactivity, and physical extinction. The Pharisees rejected their doctrine, teaching there was life after death.

The first man to believe in immortality was Job, whose faith shone brilliantly in the darkness of his surroundings (see Job 19:25).

Departed Souls . . . *Remembering*

The teaching of Jesus was concise, clear, and convincing. He insisted death was a highway to another world. That physical bodies remained in the ground was undeniable, but Christ differentiated between the body and its human tenant. When he spoke of a certain rich man, He said, "The rich man also died, and was buried: And in hell (hades), he lifted up his eyes, being in torments" (Luke 16:22–23).

Questions which are difficult to answer arise from this Scripture. The rich man's body was buried in the ground, yet afterward he spoke of fingers and tongues, and it is difficult to envisage such members without their belonging to bodies! The man was in possession of his faculties as were Abraham and Lazarus. These men were not "sleeping with their fathers!" They were not in the immediate presence of God, but in an intermediary place called Paradise (see Luke 23:43; 2 Cor. 12:4). The Lord's message suggested the place of the departed had two areas; one for the unrighteous dead; the other for those who loved and served Lord.

Delivered Saints . . . *Rejoicing*

Peter said, "David is not yet ascended into the heavens" (see Acts 2:34), and that applied to all Old Testament believers. When the Savior removed sin, He opened a way into the presence of God, proclaimed deliverance to the captives, and led a multitude of believers to heaven (see Eph. 4:8). This glorious revelation enabled Paul to speak about being "absent from the body, and to be present with the Lord" (2 Cor. 5:8). It was significant that when Christ spoke to the dying thief, He did not mention "sleeping with the fathers." The man's body was buried in a criminal's grave, but he went with Christ to "be present with the Lord."

Definite Statements . . . *Reviewed*

Teaching concerning "soul-sleep" is obsolete—Christians do not remain in their grave until the day of resurrection; they are present with Christ. Within God's realm bodies are not essential. Nevertheless, when Christ returns to earth accompanied by His saints, mortality will put on immortality. At the sound of the trump, "The dead in Christ shall rise first: Then we which are alive and remain shall be caught up together with them in the clouds, to meet the Lord in the air: and so shall we ever be with the Lord" (1 Thess. 4:16–17). That will be the greatest event in the history of the human race.

> But, Lord, 'tis for Thee;
> for Thy coming we wait;
> The sky, not the grave is our goal.

> *"And I saw heaven opened, and behold a white horse; and*
> *he that sat upon him was called Faithful and True . . . His eyes*
> *were as a flame of fire, and on his head were many crowns . . .*
> *And the armies which were in heaven followed him upon white*
> *horses, clothed in fine linen, white and clean . . . And he hath*
> *on his vesture and on his thigh a name written,*
> *KING OF KINGS, AND LORD OF LORDS" (Rev. 19:11–16).*

The most sensational event in the history of mankind will take place when a glittering procession begins at the throne of God and ends on the mount of Olives. Modern technology enables men to walk on the moon, and even children take for granted things which were ridiculed by their grandparents. Nevertheless, there are strict limitations to the accomplishments of astronauts who depend upon life-support systems and rocket-propelled vehicles. The idea of elegant riders upon white horses descending through the clouds staggers the imagination. People are accustomed to watching stars falling through space, yet only prophets inspired by God could have described events destined to amaze angels and men. In all parts of the earth, either by natural eyesight or television, nations will see a glittering procession descending to earth and watch as the King of Kings stands upon the Mount of Olives. What happens thereafter provides the most exciting reading in the Bible.

The Unchanged Christ . . . *How Thrilling*

When the Savior ascended from the Mount of Olives, angels announced He would "so come in like manner, as ye have seen him go into heaven" (Acts 1:11). The words "this same Jesus" proclaimed His unchanging immortality. The same Christ who had traversed the roads of Palestine would return to repeat His actions. He would be the same Jesus, attractive, unspeakably wonderful, ageless, and accessible. The disciples had known Him upon the earth; they would recognize Him again in the city of David. When astronauts return from space they are protected from the danger of a fiery re-entry and the gravitational pull of earth. Christ will not require such ingenuity. As He ascended slowly but surely, into the sky, so will He return. He will not need protection to offset any danger. Every force in existence will be subject to His will.

The Unchallenged Conquest . . . *How Timely*

As a contrast to the serenity of heaven, earth will be embroiled in the agony of a global war. The land of Israel will be filled with bloodshed as hostile nations try to annihilate the Jews. Two-thirds of the people will perish, but the returning Messiah will rescue one-third of His people (Zech. 13:8–9). When the Jews and their friends are threatened with disaster, God's atomic power will bring relief (Zech. 14:12), and a nation will be born in a day. God's victory will be unchallenged, for His enemies will be dead. Astonished, ashamed, but profoundly grateful, the surviving Israelis will fall at His feet. "In that day there shall be a fountain opened to the house of David and to the inhabitants of Jerusalem for sin and uncleanness" (Zech. 13:1). "And the LORD shall be king over all the earth: in that day shall there be one LORD, and his name one" (Zech. 14:9).

The Unsurpassed Coronation . . . *How Tremendous*

The nations of the world have become accustomed to the televised inauguration of United States presidents and the coronation of British monarchs. Such events will fade into insignificance when the Prince of Heaven is crowned King of Kings in Jerusalem. Daniel predicted, "And from the time that the daily sacrifice shall be taken away, and the abomination that maketh desolate set up, there shall be a thousand two hundred and ninety days" (approximately three and a half years). Daniel proceeded to say, "Blessed is he that waiteth, and cometh to the thousand three hundred and five and thirty days. But go thou thy way till the end be: for thou shalt rest, and stand in thy lot at the end of the days" (Dan. 12:11–13).

Jerusalem, which for centuries was "trodden down of the Gentiles," will become the center of earth's attention, the most glittering city in existence. The coronation of the Jewish Messiah will be almost beyond description. Even angels will rejoice when the ancient promise is fulfilled. "And, behold, thou . . . shalt call his name JESUS. He shall be great, and shall be called the Son of the Highest: and the Lord God shall give unto him the throne of his father David: And he shall reign over the house of Jacob for ever; and of his kingdom, there shall be no end" (Luke 1:31–33).

"He shall be great, and shall be called the Son of the Highest; and the Lord God shall give unto him the throne of his father David: And he shall reign over the house of Jacob for ever; and of his kingdom there shall be no end" (Luke 1:32–33).

There is an indescribable something about Jerusalem that makes it different from all other cities in the world. From the day when David captured the city of the Jebusites, the place has been the most important center in history. Jerusalem has been attacked many times and on seventeen different occasions totally destroyed. Yet it survived the onslaught of beseiging armies, and on the ashes of the past new buildings were erected. Titus and his Roman legions attacked Jerusalem in 70 A.D., and the temple was completely demolished.

The city remained under Arab control for centuries, and it was not until the end of the famous six-day war in 1967 that Jews regained control of their capital. Limitations are still imposed on the Hebrew population; they are not permitted to demonstrate nor worship in the temple area. Arab policemen patrol and guard the Mosque of Omar. Many people believe peace will never be an actual fact in Jerusalem until the Messiah solves the problems which have troubled the Middle East for centuries. The Bible reveals that God intends to make Jerusalem the greatest city in the world.

Many years ago God said to David, "And thine house and thy kingdom shall be established for ever before thee: thy throne shall be established for ever" (2 Sam. 7:16). That message was repeated when Isaiah said, "Of the increase of his government and peace there shall be no end" (Isa. 9:7). The greatest promise of all was given to Mary. God said, "And the Lord God shall give unto him the throne of his father David; And he shall reign over the house of Jacob for ever" (Luke 1:32–33). These promises have never been fulfilled; the most exciting events in time are yet to take place.

Mormons believe Christ will establish his kingdom in the United States of America, and to support their theory they refer to their own textbook which they believe to be inspired. This is common practice for exponents of non-Biblical doctrines—to rely on books thought to be more important than the Scriptures. Evidently they forget or ignore the warnings of God in Revelation 22:18–19.

A Day of Israel's Distress . . . *Problems Resolved*

Throughout the centuries, Jews endured many trials. Their greatest difficulty arose from the failure to overcome spiritual blindness inherited from ancestors. Paul said, "For the heart of this people is waxed gross, and their ears are dull of hearing, and their eyes have they closed; lest they should see with their eyes, and hear with their ears, and understand with their heart" (Acts 28:27). People who keep their eyes closed never see the light! That and other problems will be solved when Christ returns to the Mount of Olives. "In that day, shall there be a great mourning in Jerusalem . . . . And one shall say unto him, What are these wounds in thine hands? Then he shall answer, Those with which I was wounded in the house of my friends" (Zech. 12:11; 13:6).

A Day of Inspired Discovery . . . *Pardon Received*

During every major military crisis in World War II, the British government asked for a National Day of Prayer. Millions of people attended church services but never went again until the next crisis. When the nation of Israel kneels before the Messiah, Jerusalem will become a place of intense repentance and resolution. The veil which now blinds Jewish eyes will be removed, and the people will recognize "the stone which the builders rejected has become the headstone of the corner." "In that day there shall be a fountain opened to the house of David and to the inhabitants of Jerusalem for sin and for uncleanness" (Zech. 13:1). The City of David will be filled with cries of anguish, and the forgiveness of sins will be sought and obtained by every citizen.

A Day of Increasing Delight . . . *Praise Resounding*

"And the LORD shall be king over all the earth: in that day shall there be one LORD, and his name one" (Zech. 14:9). It is extremely difficult to comprehend all the wonderful things that will happen at the coronation of the Messiah. The glory of that occasion will supersede everything known in the history of mankind. "And the ransomed of the LORD shall return, and come to Zion with songs and everlasting joy upon their heads: they shall obtain joy and gladness, and sorrow and sighing shall flee away" (Isa. 35:10).

"And I saw no temple therein: for the Lord God Almighty and the Lamb are the temple of it. And the city had no need of the sun, neither of the moon, to shine in it; for the glory of God did lighten it, and the Lamb is the light thereof" (Rev. 21:22–23; see also verses 24–27).

When the Jews functioned as a nation, they always had a temple. First, there was the tabernacle in the wilderness. That was replaced by Solomon's temple, and during the Lord's ministry upon earth a restored sanctuary was the center of Israel's activities. This was destroyed by the Romans in 70 A.D. Throughout subsequent centuries, it only existed as a memory in the minds of dispersed people. Today, some of the Israeli politicians speak about the possibility of erecting a national shrine, but the cost of survival is too great to permit additional spending on a project considered by many to be unnecessary. It is thought-provoking that when the New Jerusalem descends from heaven, no temple will be within the city.

The Savior said to His disciples, "In my Father's house are many mansions; if it were not so, I would have told you. I go to prepare a place for you. And . . . I will come again, and receive you unto myself; that where I am, there ye may be also" (John 14:2–3). Evidently the special place prepared by Christ for His followers is the city that John saw descending from heaven. John described the city by highlighting its remarkable and novel "attractions."

The First Attraction . . . *No Sanctuary*

"And I saw no temple therein: for the Lord God Almighty and the Lamb are the temple of it" (v. 22). The sanctuary was always the center of attraction. It was the place where the Lord resided. Within the Holy City God will be everywhere; to seek His presence will be unnecessary. There will never be organized services; worship and praise continue indefinitely.

The Second Attraction . . . *No Sun*

"And the city had no need of the sun, neither of the moon, to shine in it: for the glory of God did lighten it, and the Lamb is the light thereof" (v. 23). John did not say there would never be sunshine; neither did he speak of the complete absence of the moon. He merely stated they would not be necessary. The city would be filled with the Shekinah glory, the sacred luminosity which comes from

173

the Lamb Himself. When Christ was upon earth He claimed to be the Light of the World. That description was inadequate—He will be the Light of every world!

The Third Attraction . . . *No Separation*

"And the gates of it shall not be shut at all by day: for there shall be no night there" (v. 25). The entrances to Biblical cities were always closed at night to provide security and defense against intruders. The only gates that remained open belonged to the cities of refuge so that no one needing refuge was prevented from entering. There will never be danger for anyone within or without God's New Jerusalem.

The Fourth Attraction . . . *No Slumber*

"There shall be no night there" (v. 25). When saints are immortal, weariness will not exist. The redeemed will be like God Who neither slumbers nor sleeps (see Ps. 121:4). This is one of the by-products of eternal life. Human bodies require rest and refreshment; even the Lord slept through a storm on the Sea of Galilee. There will never be tiredness nor exhaustion in the New Jerusalem; the Lamb will be the strength of His people.

The Fifth Attraction . . . *No Sin*

"And there shall in no wise enter into it anything that defileth, neither whatsoever worketh abomination, or maketh a lie" (v. 27). Sin will not exist, temptation will be unknown, and impurities of every kind will be eternally banished. The city and its inhabitants will be without blemish. There will be neither temple nor altar; the only indication of sacrifice will be the wound prints in the hands and side of the Lamb. The magnificent choir will sing, "Worthy is the Lamb that was slain" (Rev. 5:9, 12).

The Sixth Attraction . . . *No Strangers*

"They which are written in the Lamb's book of life" (v. 27). The people who are welcomed to the Holy City will be those who made advance reservations! They did so while they had the time and opportunity. It has been claimed that procrastination is the thief of time. People who neglect making reservations for their eternal habitations are foolish. Nothing can be as important as the salvation of a person's soul!

"Nevertheless we, according to his promise, look for new heavens and a new earth, wherein dwelleth righteousness" (2 Peter 3:13).

Throughout Jesus's ministry, the apostle Peter had a weakness. He ceased looking at Christ and became concerned with people and circumstances. When he walked on the water to go to Jesus, he saw the boisterous waves and began to sink (see Matt. 14:30). When the apostle saw and heard the people at the fire, he began to curse (see Mark 14:71). When he heard the risen Christ speaking on the beach at the Sea of Galilee, he asked questions concerning John and was politely told to mind his own business! (see John 21:21–22). When Paul considered it necessary to rebuke his colleague, it was because Peter had compromised the great truths of his message (see Gal. 2:11–13). There were occasions when Simon gave too much attention to people and not enough to the Lord. He overcame that tendency with the help of a tremendous vision that transformed his outlook. He saw the end of time and gazed by faith upon new heavens and a new earth. That entrancing sight was enough to keep his eyes open!

The Greatness of God's Power . . . *Unsurpassed*

Peter spoke of "The Day of the Lord" which would come as a thief in the night—unexpectedly, silently, and without warning. He wrote, "The heavens shall pass away with a great noise, and the elements shall melt with fervent heat, the earth also and the works that are therein shall be burned up . . . the heavens being on fire shall be dissolved, and the elements shall melt with fervent heat" (2 Peter 3:10, 12). This prediction is worthy of attention, because experiments with nuclear fission are causing concern among scientists (see the author's book, *What in the World will Happen Next?*, p. 170, Kregel Publications, Grand Rapids, MI). Sir James Jeans, the famous astronomer, said, "There are more worlds in space than there are grains of sand on all the beaches of earth," but scientists now believe he understated the facts. The universe is so large its immensity has become incomprehensible. Yet Peter believed God who will permit the lower heavens to burn but will be able to extinguish the conflagration. All parts of the outer world will remain intact and undamaged; only the lower heavens are to be destroyed. It should be remembered that when Lucifer rebelled against the Almighty, he was expelled from God's immediate presence into the lower heavens which became the headquarters of his evil administration. Those heavens, therefore, became defiled, and it will be necessary for Him to cleanse them before the world can be filled with righteousness.

The Greatness of God's Purpose . . . *Unique*

"Nevertheless we, according to his promise look for new heavens and a new earth." Theological interpretation is divided regarding the meaning of the apostle's statement. Some teachers believe that since everything, in one way or another, is indestructible, the fire will only cleanse the heavens and earth. Other theologians believe both heavens and earth will be replaced with new creations. The statement "being dissolved" suggests total destruction or at least the disappearance of that which is dissolved. This interpretation seems to be in harmony with the words of Isaiah. "For, behold, I create new heavens and a new earth: and the former shall not be remembered, nor come into mind" (Isa. 65:17). Astronomers believe that our sun belongs to a galaxy of more than a billion stars, and it is claimed there are more than one hundred billion galaxies in the universe. It is also taught that in these additional areas, there may be billions of planets similar to the earth. Since God made these worlds with a single sentence, He should have no difficulty performing the miracle described by Peter.

The Greatness of God's Pleasure . . . *Unending*

"A new earth wherein dwelleth righteousness." God's desire has never changed! When He created Adam and Eve, He commanded them to "replenish the earth." He envisaged a world of blessedness, a place without suffering, pain and death. He never planned hospitals, prisons, poverty and broken hearts. These have been the products of unrighteousness. Throughout the ages the Lord planned to do in the end times what might have been done at the beginning: to create a world filled with righteousness and happiness. There may never be another evangelistic sermon, for congregations will be filled with eternal praise. Peter saw these things; the sight so filled him with delight, he may have lost his desire to sleep!

"And I saw a great white throne, and him that sat on it, from whose face the earth and the heaven fled away; and there was found no place for them. And I saw the dead, small and great, stand before God; and the books were opened: and another book was opened which is the book of life: and the dead were judged out of those things which were written in the books, according to their works" (Rev. 20:11–12).

The promise that there will be a day of judgment received a mixed reception from innumerable people. Some, unashamedly, ridiculed it; others ignored, denied, or sought to change its message. Fools disregard it; arrogance ignores it, sinners defy it, but wise people consider it. If there be no such day, men lose nothing except their lives. If the Bible is correct, they could lose their souls. Jesus asked, "For what is a man profited, if he shall gain the whole world, and lose his own soul?" (see Matt. 16:26). If it is impossible for a man to lose his soul, Christ wasted His time speaking about sin. Every person has two appointments which cannot be canceled. The first is with death, the second with God.

The Final Call . . . *How Inescapable*

"And there was found no place for them." John saw a great white throne upon which sat the Judge of all the earth. The apostle had already written, "For the Father judgeth no man, but hath committed all judgment unto the Son" (John 5:22). That the earth and the heavens fled from His presence suggested His countenance was solemn and frightening. "His eyes were as a flame of fire" (Rev. 19:12). Even the greatest of earth's citizens fled, but no hiding place could be found—escape was impossible.

G. Franklin Allen tells that after World War II a membership roll was discovered in Germany with the names of eight million people who belonged to the Nazi party. To have one's name written in the authentic files had been a source of satisfaction, but when the war ended, everything changed. The Nazis fled in all directions, but for many there were no hiding places. They were extradited from other countries, taken back to Nuremberg, and sentenced for their crimes. That might be an illustration of the end of time; no one will be able to escape from the far-reaching arm of divine law.

The Factual Consideration . . . *How Irrefutable*

"And the dead were judged out of those things which were written in the books, according to their works." Perhaps John referred to "books" because he had no knowledge of computers! The world has grown accustomed to machines that are capable of carrying the records of all people. Are there computers in heaven? God knew about them even from the beginning, and it may be beyond comprehension what angels can do in compiling the records of sinners who reject the overtures of the Almighty. The Savior spoke about a man who was speechless when asked by a king to explain his unpardonable behavior (see Matt. 22:12). Christ then described how the sinner was expelled from the king's presence and there was "weeping and gnashing of teeth." The implications of that story were easily recognized; they related to the time when guilty people will be required to explain why they refused to accept God's wedding garment of salvation.

The Fatal Condemnation . . . *How Irreversible*

"And whosoever was not found written in the book of life was cast into the lake of fire" (Rev. 20:15). There is no court of appeal in eternity. Here on earth retribution may be delayed for years because there are courts which consider appeals for clemency. When God pronounces sentence upon sinners, they are condemned forever; their guilt is established beyond doubt. Some theologians believe eternal doom means annihilation, that the punishment is eternal in effect only. Others teach sinners will be eternally separated from God, heaven, hope, and everything desirable. Whatever the final interpretation may be, the price is too high to be paid for the pleasures of this world. God offers pardon for every sin, a permanent home in heaven, and the assurance of eternal life. The Savior said, "Verily, verily, I say unto you. He that heareth my word, and believeth on him that sent me, hath everlasting life, and shall not come into condemnation; but is passed from death unto life" (John 5:24). A dying Christian astronomer said, "There is no need to fear the night if you live with the stars."

"Then cometh the end, when he shall have delivered up the kingdom to God, even the Father; when he shall have put down all rule, and all authority and power. For he must reign till he hath put all enemies under his feet. The last enemy that shall be destroyed is death . . . And when all things shall be subdued unto him, then shall the Son also himself be subject unto him that put all things under him, that God may be all and in all" (1 Cor. 1:24–28).

The revelation of truth given to Paul enabled the apostle to see the end from the beginning. During his long and exacting ministry he endured many trials, but he never wavered in his faith of what would happen at the end of time. He knew Satan and sin would win occasional battles, but the final victory belonged to God. Nations would arise and exercise frightening power, but ultimately they would cease to exist. The authority of God would be challenged, but righteousness would not only survive, it would continue eternally. The letter to the Corinthian church explained what Paul believed, and that document remains one of the most cherished pieces of literature.

The Greatest Enemy . . . *Annihilated*

Throughout the ages, death continued to be man's greatest foe. Diseases thought to be incurable were overcome, and innumerable lives prolonged. Leprosy, polio, tuberculosis and other scourges were checked by scientific research, but death was only delayed. From the time when Adam and Eve looked at their murdered son (see Gen. 4:8) to the present time when cemeteries can be found in every nation, death has been a tyrant, destroying happiness and ruining lives. Innocent children, famous scientists, royalty and peasants became victims. When Christ challenged and overcame the power of death, many people refused to believe the impossible had happened. Writing to his friends in Corinth, Paul insisted, "If Christ be not risen, then is our preaching vain, and your faith is also vain" (1 Cor. 15:14). The apostle explained how the resurrection of the Savior was only a part of the purpose of God. Christ was "the firstfruits" (see 1 Cor. 15:23) of a great harvest. Ultimately, death would not even exist; it would die! Throughout future ages there would never be need for hospitals, doctors, funeral parlors, nor cemeteries! Death which had cast shadows over the first world would never again threaten the happiness of God's people.

The Greatest Act . . . *Abdication*

"For he (Christ) must reign, till he hath put all enemies under his feet . . . then shall the Son also himself be subject unto him that put all things under him." Paul did not suggest that the Lord would disappear from the eternal scene. Voluntarily, the Son had accepted an assignment given by the Father, but when His redemptive responsibilities had been fulfilled, He was free to accept the accolade of heaven. Thereafter, His greatest desire would be to spend eternity with His bride. As the Father had watched the Son completing His mission, so, throughout eternity, the Lord would watch and appreciate His church, the Lamb would continue to reside in the city which the apostle saw descending from heaven (see Rev. 1:10–27). Describing that city, John said the streets were paved with gold! Was he suggesting that earth's most valuable commodity would become so commonplace that heaven's citizens would walk on it?

The Greatest Goal . . . *Achieved*

"That God may be all and in all." Man's mind is too undeveloped to comprehend the unfathomable depths of Paul's statement. Redeemed souls are not destined to become dummies or robots. Decisions will be made, actions planned, and successes won, but throughout eternity God will be present with His people. Every provision made by the Almighty will fill His people with amazement. God has never revealed everything to happen in the hereafter, but evidently there will be new occupations. If this were not so, gravediggers and funeral directors would be unemployed forever! There will never be armament factories nor steel mills producing the paraphernalia of war. Isaiah's words will be literally fulfilled, "They shall not hurt nor destroy in all my holy mountain: for the earth shall be full of the knowledge of the LORD, as the waters cover the sea" (Isa. 11:9). "And they shall beat their swords into plowshares, and the spears into pruninghooks: nation shall not lift sword against nation, neither shall they learn war any more" (Isaiah 2:4). God will indeed be "All and in all."

"And they shall see his face; and his name shall be in their foreheads" (Rev. 22:4).

When I was a young Christian I listened to a strange old man whose prayer seemed quaint and yet wonderful. He said, "O God, I thank thee I never had wings! If I had, I would be up there tormenting Thee day and night and would probably be sent down here again." I was intrigued by his expressions, but the people in the prayer meeting knew exactly what Henry Richards meant. He believed heaven was so wonderful that had he possessed the ability to fly, he would have gone there immediately. That man was approaching ninety years of age, but his prayer was unforgettable. The saints in heaven will walk on streets of gold, explore the Holy City, meet many people, sing the praises of the Lamb, and see woundprints in the hands and side of the Savior. Yet, to see the face of Jesus will provide the greatest of all thrills.

A Dangerous Vision . . . *Exodus 33:20*

When the redeemed see their Lord, it will be the superlative climax to their earthly pilgrimage. To appreciate its magnitude, it is necessary to consider certain Scriptures. When Moses communed with the Lord in Mount Sinai, the Lord said, "Thou canst not see my face: for there shall no man see me and live." God was not implying that He desired to live in everlasting obscurity, nor suggesting that humans would never be permitted to draw near to their Maker. Israel had not witnessed a complete manifestation of God's glory, and the outshining of eternal holiness might have been fatal to sinful people. Moses was placed in "the cleft in the rock" to see God's "back parts" (see Ex. 33:21–23). Had man tried to do what was forbidden, ensuing judgment would have been disastrous.

A Definite Virtue . . . *2 Corinthians 4:6*

Against the background of Sinai's prohibition, the words of Jesus shine as a brilliant star. Christ said, "Blessed are the pure in heart: for they shall see God" (Matt. 5:8). The Lord indicated the closed door was beginning to open! If people were pure in heart, someday they would see the Almighty. Yet, even God knew complete purity of heart was not within reach of sinners. Therefore, the Savior said to Philip, "He that hath seen me hath seen the Father; and how sayest thou then, Shew us the Father?" (John 14:9). If it were not possible for sinners to see God, at least they knew what He was like! In reply to the question, What is God like?, the answer was contained in one word—Jesus.

A Desperate Venture . . . *Revelation 6:15–16*

When John described the events to precede the day of judgment, he used impressive words, "And the kings of the earth, and the great men, and the rich men, and the chief captains, and the mighty men, and every bondman, and every free man, hid themselves in the dens, and in the rocks of the mountains; And said to the mountains and rocks, Fall on us, and hide us from the face of him that sitteth on the throne, and from the wrath of the Lamb." It should never be forgotten that God hates sin as much as He loves sinners! Redemption provided means whereby guilty people could approach the throne of grace. If the way—the Savior—were rejected and ignored, the wrath suggested on Mount Sinai would become operative, and guilty people would perish.

A Delightful Victory . . . *Revelation 22:4*

The only attractive detail about the Cross was its shape! It was, so to speak, God's signpost. A part pointed toward heaven; the lower end reached to earth, and the two arms indicated different directions. The unrepentant sinner followed the road which led to tragedy, the other thief the way by which men could find forgiveness and peace. The distance between the two extremes was measureless. At the end of one road men fear the wrath of the Lamb, and endeavor to flee from His presence. At the other terminal, redeemed souls gaze in wonder at the face of the Redeemer and prepare to sing His praise throughout eternity. People must decide which direction they desire to take. Their decision in time will be final in eternity. It will be impossible to change directions after death has closed the door of opportunity.

> Someday my earthly house will fall,
> I cannot tell how soon 'twill be;
> But this I know—my All in All,
> Has now a place in heav'n for me.
> And I shall see Him face to face
> And tell the story—Saved by grace.

SCRIPTURE INDEX

183

184

186

Books by Ivor Powell

Bible Cameos
Vivid biographies of 80 Bible characters graphically portrayed. Full of
helps and hints for sermon preparation.
ISBN 0-8254-3515-3   **192 pp.**   **paperback**

Bible Gems
Preachers will enjoy an ample supply of sermon starters, teachers will
find many illustrations, and laymen will be led to the deep truths of
God's Word as Powell traces 80 various Bible themes.
ISBN 0-8254-3527-7   **176 pp.**   **paperback**

Bible Highways
This volume transports the reader through a variety of over 40 themes
found in the Scriptures and then provides over 90 rich illustrations to
communicate the message effectively. Valuable material for the pastor
or teacher in a pulpit or teaching ministry.
ISBN 0-8254-3521-8   **176 pp.**   **paperback**

Bible Names of Christ
The author, in his gifted manner, presents 80 short studies on the
names and titles of Christ. The simplicity and freshness of these mini-
messages will provide enlightening devotional studies for believers
and many outlines and illustrations for teachers and preachers.
ISBN 0-8254-3530-7   **176 pp.**   **paperback**

Bible Nuggets
These 34 insightful studies of Bible characters provide enjoyable and
challenging reading for pastors and teachers alike.
ISBN 0-8254-3512-9   **192 pp.**   **paperback**

Bible Pinnacles
Over 80 detailed character sketches, pivotal incidents, miracles, and parables. Excellent homiletical helps. "Powell pours his rich treasure, amassed in the course of his world-wide preaching experience, into the hungry hearts of his eager readers." *–F.W. Boreham*
ISBN 0-8254-3516-1   **192 pp.**   **paperback**

Bible Windows
A rich collection of over 80 carefully chosen illustrations to better communicate the gospel message and bring to life the key points of its message.
ISBN 0-8254-3522-6   **180 pp.**   **paperback**

Distinctively Different Commentaries Series. In an exciting, different style, Powell presents vivid illustrations and alliterative outlines which blend exposition and rich spiritual insight. To read and study his writings is to embark on a thrilling journey. Full of practical teaching and preaching helps.

Matthew's Majestic Gospel
ISBN 0-8254-3544-7   **526 pp.**   **paperback**

Mark's Superb Gospel
ISBN 0-8254-3510-2   **432 pp.**   **paperback**

Luke's Thrilling Gospel
ISBN 0-8254-3513-7   **508 pp.**   **hardback**

John's Wonderful Gospel
ISBN 0-8254-3514-5   **446 pp.**   **hardback**

The Amazing Acts
ISBN 0-8254-3526-9   **478 pp.**   **hardback**

The Exciting Epistle to the Ephesians
ISBN 0-8254-3537-4   **304 pp.**   **hardback**

DAVID: His Life and Times
David, the "sweet psalmist of Israel," comes alive in a unique and refreshing manner, typical of Ivor Powell's writings. Provides a biographical commentary on David's life and times as well as devotional studies, outlines, and illustrations for teachers and preachers.
ISBN 0-8254-3532-3   **448 pp.**   **paperback**

What in the World Will Happen Next?
A scripturally sound work which effectively describes the important prophetic events yet to be fulfilled. The book offers a wealth of material in the author's popular style on this fascinating and increasingly studied subject.
ISBN 0-8254-3524-2   **176 pp.**   **paperback**